the longest road

For Allison

the longest road

Finding Peace With the Past

Maureen Lyttle

Canadian Cataloguing in Publication Data
Lyttle, Maureen
    The Longest Road: Finding Peace with the Past / by Maureen Lyttle

Includes bibliographical references and index.
ISBN 0-9730944-0-0

    1. Lyttle, Maureen.   2. Single mothers—Biography.
    3. Children of single parents—Family relationships.   I. Title.
HQ759.915.L97 2002   362.82'94'092   C2002-910567-6

Elaine Kenney of Communication Matters, Ottawa acted as publishing consultant on the book, offering editorial comment and valuable input at many levels.

Cover photograph by Maureen Lyttle
Design by Icon Communications
Published in Canada by The Longest Road Publishing
    P.O. Box 34046
    1610 – 37th Street S.W.
    Calgary, Alberta T3C 3W2
    thelongestroad@telus.net

First Printing 2002

Printed and bound in Canada by Transcontinental Printing

Dedication

This book is dedicated to my dear sister Deirdre, who suffered much in her life and had the courage to take the journey home with me. This book could not have been written without her.

Contents

Foreword

"The longest road out is the shortest road home."
Old Irish Saying

As spiritual beings on the human quest of life, we are offered unique experiences, opportunities and paths leading us to the healing journey. One such unique life experience is the search for our "birthright" and "reunification" with what was lost, never certain of what will be found. Maureen Lyttle's profound and complex story and inner journey is a testimony to courage, trust, faith and wisdom of the soul, as the darkness of the past is embraced and released.

Maureen's journey is the "coming home to self" and finally living her birthright of peace, freedom and joy! It was an honour to walk beside you, as you entered your journey into the light. I celebrate and honour your story, and I highly commend and recommend this testimony for all those seeking to be whole and free.

Living now in Hawaii, Colleen E. Clark, MSW, RSW, is a Clinical Social Worker who continues to write, provides workshops, and is in clinical trauma healing practice, as she continues to specialize in reunification, adoption and birth family issues. She can be reached at: imagine_colleen@yahoo.com

Acknowledgments

I wish to acknowledge the following special people:

Dr. Narsui, my doctor, whose extraordinary compassion and gentle guidance and support proved invaluable in the very difficult process of recovery from trauma and mental illness.

Colleen Clark, my therapist, whose incredible wisdom and experience as a trauma specialist led me through the darkness into the light.

My good friends, for their tremendous encouragement and loving help and support through this most difficult time in my life.

— Maureen Lyttle

1 *The Primal Wound*[1]

My father died when I was six years old. My mother, eight months pregnant with my father's tenth child, buried him and never spoke of him again. What I did not realize that day, nor would I fully comprehend for the next thirty-four years, was that she also buried all nine of her surviving children. We were just too close to her pain. We would all survive, of course, but the damage would be, for the most part, irreparable.

I remember the day as if it were yesterday.

It was a hot, sunny day in June. We had driven to the hospital, a neighbour and my mother in the front seat, and my younger sister Kathy, then four years old, in the back with me. My mother and the neighbour got out in a hurry, leaving my sister and me alone. As time went by, I felt anxious and overly warm in the back seat of the old car. I did not understand, nor could I possibly comprehend, the tragic event that had just taken place within the confines of the hospital. My little sister squirmed beside me, wanting to get out. We were both restless, and I began to feel very uncomfortable and distressed, waiting for mother to return. Finally, after what seemed at eternity, they reappeared. Slumped over and weeping uncontrollably, my mother stumbled towards the car, supported on either side by a stranger. I was terrified seeing my mother like this and desperately needed an explanation as to what had happened. Not a word was forthcoming.

She stooped to enter the car and smashed her head against the door frame. I sat there, dazed, thinking how much that must have hurt and why didn't she cry out in pain. My younger sister whimpered beside me, and I held on to her tightly. Something very important had just happened, and I had to try hard to remember this. It would affect me the rest of my life. Try as I might, I cannot remember the car ride home.

We were gathered in the living room, and everyone was deathly quiet. My brothers and sisters had been taken out of school, and we all stood awkwardly about, confused and not knowing what to do. There was a neighbour in the room with us, which was heavy with gloom and semi-dark. No one thought to turn on a light. There were none of the usual sounds of supper being prepared coming from the kitchen. A strange and eery silence permeated the old house as darkness enveloped us. We huddled with the two youngest children, who cried in vain for their mother. She was weeping in the next room, but we were restrained from seeing her. I wandered from room to room, talking to myself, numb with shock. Still no one comforted me.

A few days later we were dressed in our Sunday best, bonnets and all, and taken to the funeral home where my father was laid out. He was pasty-looking, and when I was held up to kiss him a final good-bye, he was cold and stiff to the touch. I didn't cry. Nor did I understand why some of the relatives were weeping and making such a fuss. I was traumatized over these proceedings and remained silent. Perhaps they thought I was too young to understand. In any event, I had been forgotten, and no one bothered to tell me he had died.

The others knew. I stood quietly in the church next to my older sister Patricia, who was eight at the time. She was crying broken heartedly.

"Why aren't you crying?" she demanded of me, painfully jabbing me in the side with her elbow. "You're supposed to be crying!"

I stood there, confused and numb with shock, unable to utter a word.

I do not remember any gravesite service, nor do I remember the days that followed. In fact, I don't remember much of anything else except being very much alone that summer.

I didn't miss him. He was rarely home anyway, and occasionally I witnessed him coming home late in a state of drunkenness, and it terrified me. I didn't know at the time he was intoxicated or what that actually was or why he fell on the floor, unable to get up. I was quickly ushered back to bed with a lollipop for comfort. My mother and older brothers helped him into bed and nothing was ever said about it. I couldn't understand why I got a special treat for witnessing him drunk.

Mostly, my father spent time with his boys working on the old Studebaker in the backyard. He never spent time with me, except on one occasion that I can remember. He was working on an old engraving machine in the basement, making broaches with Royal Air Force inscriptions engraved into them. I watched in wonderment as the swirl of brightly-coloured paint was carefully placed into the carving. I felt special standing next to him, intently watching him work. I did not realize at the time that he was an artist, and later on in my life, I would become one as well. I did not have to have dinner with the rest of my siblings upstairs when mother called down to me.

"She's with me, mother!" he answered. Indeed, those few precious moments would never leave my memory, for he never spent time with me again. A massive heart attack claimed his life shortly thereafter.

Summer came and went. I played alone or with my younger sister Kathy. Mother had given birth just one month earlier and was extremely busy with the tenth baby. All of her time was spent with Josephine. Although I felt very much alone, I never complained. Instead, Kathy and I were free to roam and occupied ourselves running across 17th Avenue, the busy roadway that ran from the city core to the poorer outskirts on the southeastern edge of the city. The road ran right in front of our dilapidated, old house with the run-down, weather-beaten fence. I held Kathy's hand, and we ran across the road, laughing. When traffic cleared, we similarly darted back to the other side, breathless and laughing harder. Many times we did this, each time finding it more exhilarating than the last. We had discovered a new game—playing on the road, in the traffic.

A police car approached.

"Where do you live?" one of the officers demanded of me in a very stern voice.

Afraid to speak, I pointed across the road. Unfortunately, we were caught on the wrong side of the street.

"Get on home and don't run across the road again!" was the strict admonishment.

The blood crept into my face, and for the first time in my very young life, I felt shame. My sister and I scampered back across the road, and as I nervously glanced back over my shoulder, I saw the police car drive away slowly, checking our progress. *Time for a new game, Kathy. No, we can't run back across the street. Why not? Just because.*

When I was older and recalled this memory I would laugh, but there would come a time when I cried like a baby, wondering why on earth a six-year-old child was taking care of a four-year-old. Who the hell was taking care of me? I was, in effect, at the tender young age of six, my own little parent.

Because I had not yet received my First Holy Communion, I would sometimes be allowed to stay home from Sunday mass. I delighted in making the beds and tidying the house, as best a six-year-old can do. In my young mind, I thought it would make my mother happy. But it never worked.

Those two months after my father's death were the loneliest of my young life.

I looked forward with anticipation to my first day of school and getting away from the sadness that permeated the place called home. Finally, the first day of school arrived. I was able to find my class and approached my grade one teacher, Mother Gemma, with trepidation. I had never seen a nun before and her black habit scared me. She asked me several questions and finally asked me about my father. Remembering my mother's careful instructions of the previous night, I answered her nervously:

"He passed away."

I wasn't even sure what the words meant. I only knew he was gone. After that day, I became the teacher's pet. At least once a week, Mother Gemma would collect all the sweet desserts from the teachers during lunch hour, put them in a white box tied with string and keep me after class. She would give me the treats and tell me to take them home to share with my brothers and sisters. Dutifully, I wouldn't eat any of them but would bring them all home to my mother. I would gleefully present them to her, so very proud of my accomplishment, thinking: *This will surely make her happy!* But it never worked. She stayed sad.

We were poor and lived on welfare. Word quickly spread throughout the parish that a family of ten fatherless children had just immigrated from Belfast, Northern Ireland. At two separate Sunday church services, the congregation took up a collection for a down payment for a house for my mother, and we moved into our new home shortly thereafter.

All of mother's attention was focused on the new baby. She was an adorable child, but mother spoilt her rotten, taking her side in every squabble. Gradually, we all began to dislike Josephine as she became more and more undisciplined and a first-rate brat. She always got her way by crying to mother. And mother always took her side. We got used to mother's favoritism and dismissed it, each of us silent about it and secretly knowing why mother behaved this way. What mother didn't seem to realize, however, was that we needed her too. I remember years later asking her why she had had so many babies, and her answer troubled me.

"They make you feel so needed."

Needed? I stared at her questioningly. She explained, "They cling to you and make you feel so needed. Then they can walk, and they don't need you anymore."

Don't need you anymore? Time for another baby—to feel needed all over again? Good God. So once you hit one and a half to two years of age, you no longer need a mother? I was silently enraged with her but didn't argue. You didn't argue with mother. It would be a long time before I had the knowledge of psychology to understand the dysfunctional aspect of her behaviour and realize that she herself had been narcissistically deprived by her own mother, my grandmother. I only knew at the time that her words distressed and angered me deeply.

To bear children to feel needed.

Small as we were, we slept three to a bed. I could still hear the muffled sounds of my mother's anguish coming from her bedroom night after night, behind her bedroom door. She tried to hide the sounds of her pain in the cloth she held tightly to her face, but I could still hear her. Sometimes I accidentally opened that door and found her rocking back and forth, always with that cloth to her face, in a futile attempt to stifle the agonizing moans that escaped her. It distressed me profoundly to see her in such pain and to witness her terrible suffering, but at six years of age, I was too young to know what to do or how to help. Later on in my life, I often thought that if my mother had just shared her grief with us, we could have expressed ours, and we would have grieved together. Surely, that's what families do. But that would not happen, at least not for the next five years.

Finally, on a beautiful, warm, sunny day, she took us to the gravesite. There was a marker in the ground but no headstone. Welfare recipients were not given money for headstones, so my father never got one. The six of us girls, the youngest five, stood solemnly around the grave marker, crying. Josephine, the youngest, could not understand why we were all weeping and, bewildered, demanded of us, "Why are you crying?" As we stared at one other, someone accidentally giggled and we erupted into gales of laughter. It felt good to laugh, even if it was at poor Josephine's expense. Josephine tightly held a big bag of chocolate chip cookies Mom had made and we passed them around. On the way home, Mom bought us cokes. Such a luxury—I knew she couldn't afford cokes—but she must have known we needed something special that day. For the first time since my father's death, we had been allowed to grieve, and it felt good.

A few months later, my eldest sister Deirdre, on our behalf, nervously approached my mother.

"Mom, we'd like to go back and visit the gravesite." The two of them were in the kitchen, and I listened intently for her answer from the bedroom. My mother's words cut sharply through the air like a knife.

"No! They've moved the grave, and no one knows where it is."

I felt as if a nuclear blast had just exploded and rocked the room. *Oh God! They've moved the grave? Where did it go?* I was numb with shock. I had never heard of anyone losing a grave. But of course we believed mother. We were just kids.

That night my nightmares began. Night after night, I awoke in a cold sweat with a paralyzing scream stuck in my throat. During those terrifying night terrors, I searched through graveyards for a grave that was no longer there. The people who kept the records of the dead in the graves had destroyed them and in my dream I continued to wander aimlessly, searching again and again for my father's grave. Just eleven years old, I would be haunted by the nightmares for the next fifteen years. I was too young to realize they were a symptom of unresolved grief that desperately needed to be put to rest. Finally, in my teen years, with the discovery of drugs, I found a way to stay wide awake at night and silence the terrifying dreams. I had found a way to endure.

Certainly, there were a few happy times in those first years after his death. Mother took us for picnics and outings to Chestermere Lake, an irrigation canal really, a few miles outside of town. There was no development there at the time except an old road that ran off the main highway down to an even older broken-down store with a large *Coke* sign out front and the water's edge. But to us children, it was paradise. We laughed and played together in the seaweed-infested water, jumping off the dock. When we got hungry, mother would have prepared a tantalizing feast of baked stuffed chicken, buns, watermelon and potato salad that we partook of ravenously. As the day wore on and night began to fall, the giant poplar trees rustled in the wind and the air cooled. It was time to go home. Scant though they were, I would never forget those days at Chestermere Lake.

Mother was a marvelous cook, being Ukrainian, and she baked all the time. Throughout my childhood, I enjoyed watching her make bread, buns or cinnamon rolls on the old, cracked marble table in the kitchen. I loved the delicate aroma of freshly baked bread and buns hot from the oven that wafted through the air and escaped the kitchen. She would melt a little butter on the steaming loaves and buns and let them cool. One thing my mother did manage to do was to instill in each of us an incredible love of the outdoors and cooking.

Nor was there ever a lack of us kids to play a good game of hide-and-seek, tag or evi-ivy-over. My brothers were all older than me and they joined in. Sometimes we played well past dusk until the sound of mother's voice, carried through the night air, called us to come home. I did receive some measure of comfort from my siblings in those early years, but it was the only time that we ever managed to get along.

Unfortunately, it was not enough. As children, we may have played together, but a very fundamental need was lacking. Mother managed to provide the material necessities for life, but she was unable to provide the love, nurturing and guidance we all so desperately needed. Emotionally, my mother was destroyed. She had stayed in her grief over the loss of my father. It was as if a giant, black shroud had been draped over the entire house, keeping everyone in it immersed in eternal sadness. I often thought it was more like living in a coffin.

As time went on and we entered our teenage years, mother remained isolated and immersed in her sadness and grief, and our grief remained unexpressed and unresolved. Without being told, we knew to leave it alone. Unable to express her emotions or feelings, there were little or no intimate moments with her. In time, I became very distanced and estranged from this emotionally crippled woman, my mother. Unable to speak intimately about her thoughts, her feelings, her life, her hopes and her dreams, I was denied the opportunity of knowing who she really was. Nor did she ever mention my father to me. Her ability to love, drastically diminished. I came to realize that the day my father died was the day my mother died as well. She cooked, she cleaned and she dressed us, but emotionally, we all felt severe neglect.

Eventually, my mother's initial grief at her husband's death turned to rage and I grew terrified of her. She exploded at each of us, excluding the youngest. Unfortunately, my eldest sister Deirdre received the worst of mother's rage. Mother whipped her with belts, straps and rubber skipping ropes that left swollen, black and blue marks and large, raised welts across Deirdre's arms and legs almost daily. Deirdre would stand there—angry, defiant, resolute.

"You're not going to make me cry!"

So mother continued thrashing her, determined to break her spirit. Deirdre never broke down, and the rest of us cowered or hid, terrified of receiving the same punishment. Deirdre braved the beatings, and I wanted so desperately for her to shut up so mother would stop. But Deirdre never shut up, and mother never stopped beating her. My brother Brian encouraged mother to beat Deirdre into submission, telling mother that it was the only way to control Deirdre. I hated my brother for that.

Amazingly, that same brother, Brian, was the child my mother blamed for my father's death. He was only fifteen at the time, and mother admitted to me years later she had shouted at Brian shortly after my father's death:

"It's your fault your father died! You fought with him all the time! You killed him! You killed your father!"

Brian became, through the years, so far removed from his emotions that no one could adequately express any feeling or emotion to him. Instead, he called himself an 'intellectual.' There was simply no room for emotions in his life—emotions he would never be able to handle.

I wondered then, how in God's name at the time of my father's death could Brian, a fifteen-year-old boy so unjustly accused of killing his father, then callously encourage the beating of his own sister? Another brother, Joe, was equally insensitive, snickering whenever Deirdre was beaten. He took gleeful pleasure in watching Mom whip her again and again. I often caught Mom snickering herself, as if there was a pleasure to be derived from administering such brutal punishment. Deirdre never flinched, but stood staunchly resolute, determined not to cry or break. Even more horrendously, mother would not stop the lashing until her arm was too tired to wield yet another blow. I couldn't understand for the life of me how such God-awful violent behaviour could be exacted by my own mother. I hated her for that.

In an act of angry determination, Mom yanked Deirdre out of school, placed her in a detention home and made her a ward of the government. In effect, she took away the only security and stability that poor Deirdre had ever known in her short, miserable life. School, friends—her only source of strength and identity—all snatched from her. I don't know if Deirdre ever fully recovered from this. In witnessing my eldest sister being flogged, I became a victim as well, but it would be my sister who would have to bear the painful physical and emotional scars for the rest of her life. Her spirit would be broken for the next thirty years, and it would require years of therapy for her to begin to recover that beautiful, resilient spirit and hellishly damaged self-esteem.

The pain, indelibly etched into Deirdre's soul, was evident as she asked me recently in a sad and broken voice:

"Maureen, what did I do that was so bad that I was beaten every day of my life?"

I tried to explain that mother had taken out all her unresolved pain and anger on her eldest daughter because Deirdre reminded mother of her own pain and shame. I knew my words were of little comfort to my sister, but I loved her and had to try.

I didn't totally escape my mother's brutality either. As the family grew increasingly troubled, the fighting amongst us increased in intensity. It was a violent household, but for all intents and purposes, we appeared to the outside world as a normal, healthy family. Little did they know. My mother's only method of control was violence—with her hand, a belt and those damn skipping ropes. Those rubber ropes stung sharply, leaving ugly, swollen welts on the recipient of the blows. *Why didn't she just speak to us? Why couldn't she simply admonish us for what we had done wrong? Why did she have to use violence?*

On one occasion, my mother used a metal sword to give me a whack. By now, I had had enough of mother's shameful beating nonsense. I exploded with rage and screamed at her:

"You're trying to kill me! Go ahead—kill me!"

She stopped dead in her tracks, stunned and completely taken aback at my thunderous outburst. She tittered nervously, as if still in control of the situation, but at that moment, my mother lost her power over me. I was no longer afraid of her. Although she would never hit me again, she would find other methods in an attempt to control me.

As with my sister, she failed miserably.

The family unit continued to deteriorate.

Money was scarce, so I began babysitting to make a few extra dollars. I was thirteen years old when it happened.

It was a freezing cold winter night in January. The temperature had dropped to -40°F and I was stuck indoors. Although the King children, a young girl, nine years old, and a young boy, seven, were undisciplined and difficult to manage, when the call came that evening to babysit, I was happy to oblige and escape the isolation of home. Mr. King picked me up and drove me to the outskirts of the city. His house was in the last street of development, and across the road, grasses in the fields were frozen over and stuck up through the snow drifts. Everything was frozen solid.

Before Mr. and Mrs. King left me alone with the children, Mrs. King told me that her brother-in-law was staying with them downstairs and not to be afraid if I heard him come in the back door. They left, and, as usual, I had a trying time with the two children. A cuckoo clock kept meticulous time on the kitchen wall, and when the little bird chirped nine times, it was the children's bedtime. It took me over an hour to get them off to bed, using every method of persuasion I could think of. Unfortunately, the little fellow had learned to tell time and refused to go to bed until 10 p.m. Finally, I succeeded in getting them to bed and, exhausted, was able at last to relax. They were a handful, those two youngsters. I checked on them every so often. They were fast asleep.

The bird chirped twelve times. It was midnight, and feeling restless with very little on the T.V. to watch, I walked over to the dining room window and peered outside. The wind howled in the streets and snow was blowing and collecting in drifts. A movement just outside the window startled me, and I jumped with fright. There was a man walking just underneath the window. I caught a glimpse of his Russian-style hat with short, curly fur on his head as he passed by. My heart skipped a beat and I began to panic. *Calm down—it's only the brother-in-law—the fellow who lives downstairs.* I tried desperately to calm my racing heartbeat when I heard the key turn in the lock and his thumping boots descending the stairs. I sat rigid on the couch, unnerved and shaken.

Minutes passed. As I listened intently, I could hear his muffled movements downstairs. My heart began to pound again when I heard him ascending the stairs. The kitchen door leading to the basement opened. I was surprised that he had come upstairs and nervously listened to his footsteps approaching through the kitchen. He appeared in the doorway—tall, lanky and not very good-looking. He said hello, sat down and began small talk with me.

I started to relax a little and answered questions about school and such. Then he asked me to come over to him. Without a lot of hesitation, and innocent and unsuspecting as I was, I walked over to where he was sitting on a chair against the wall. Without warning, he grabbed me and pulled me onto his lap, my back to him. He held me firmly, one strong arm around my chest, and the other around my waist, pinning my arms to my side. Terrified, I froze and was unable to scream. His hand slid down between my legs, and he roughly rubbed it back and forth over my genitals. The other hand crudely maneuvered to my chest, and he roughly handled my small breasts. I wanted to scream but couldn't. *If I screamed and woke the children, he would go after the little girl.* I felt overwhelming terror at what he was doing to me. An eternity passed and my terror escalated. He continued to rub his hands hard over my body. Still no scream would escape my lips. I was petrified to death.

Suddenly, the word *rape* flashed in my mind. *Better he rape me than that little nine-year-old girl asleep in the bedroom. I could survive it—the little girl surely wouldn't.*

Just as suddenly, I felt a movement in his groin beneath my buttocks, and he relaxed his powerful grip on me. In one swift, violent motion, I lunged forward, broke free of his hold and bolted to the door. I flung it wide open, ready to flee. I wanted to run yelling and screaming down the street, waking up the entire block, but I couldn't. Heart pounding, I stopped dead in my tracks in the open doorway.

Never leave the children alone. Don't ever leave the children. It was mother's voice. *Oh God, how could I leave those two little ones with this monster? I thought in horror.* The door was wide open and the freezing cold air rushed in. I stood there, defiant, ready to bolt at a moment's notice if he made the slightest move towards me.

Shaking uncontrollably, I was enraged at this bastard who had so crudely and so terrifyingly sexually molested me.

"Come on back inside," he said in a detached voice as if nothing had happened.

"No." He could hear the controlled anger in my voice.

"Come on back inside, you must be freezing cold."

"No, I'm fine right here." *I was freezing to death.*

Whatever you do, don't desert the children! Don't go back inside! I glared at him fiercely from the open doorway, breathing heavily, fury pulsating every nerve of my body. *I could stand here all night if I had to. I would let out a death-curdling scream if he moved one inch from that chair.*

"Come on back in. I promise not to touch you."

"Are you sure?" I demanded.

"Yes. We can play cards. Do you know how to play cards?"

"Yes."

As a sign of good faith, he got up and came back with a deck of cards and sat on a chair next to the coffee table. I watched him as he shuffled the deck and dealt the cards with indifference. Sensing that he wouldn't touch me again and that he was no longer a threat, I quietly shut the door, moved tentatively towards the couch and sat opposite him. We played several hands of gin rummy.

The clock ticked on.

Finally, they came home. Mrs. King asked me if everything went okay. I glared at *him* and felt the powerful and penetrating look in his eyes, daring me to tell.

The putrid son-of-a-bitch. I lied. "Everything was fine."

Mr. King drove me home. I did not tell my mother what had happened. I knew she would never let me out of the house again, and in any event, it was all my fault. I shouldn't have gone over to him when he beckoned me to. He not only stole my innocence that night, but also my childhood.

I never babysat at the King's house again.

2 *Escape From Reality*

I entered high school and spent most of my time away from home, playing badminton at school morning, noon and night. There was little or nothing to do at home, so school and friends became an escape for me. A wonderful escape.

Mary-Ann was my best friend in high school, and throughout grade 10, we became inseparable. People got us so confused they often called me Maury-Ann. My close friendship with her helped me cope with some of the most difficult years of my life, unable to escape a violent, severely co-dependent family life. My only desire was to flee that life, and I would make excuses at every waking moment to do so. Home was not where I wanted to be. Surely, I was not living a normal, healthy life, and somewhere deep inside me, I knew it.

During the course of the year, Mary-Ann met Gary and began dating him. Gary, in turn, introduced us to his friend, Cary. The four of us spent much of grade 10 together, outside of classes. Mary-Ann and I went to St. Mary's girl school, just two blocks from the boy's school. Needless to say, we were always at the boy's school. Cary was in grade 12 and two years my senior. I felt rather important, being with these older fellows. I was barely sixteen. Cary was extremely handsome, and although we never dated, I enjoyed his company immensely.

On one occasion Cary invited us to his brother's apartment, but the landlady took one look at us and refused to let us in. So Cary purchased a bottle of vodka and we sat on the grass in a nearby park and proceeded to guzzle it. Mary-Ann and I drank the entire bottle between us and made total assholes of ourselves—I, in my short dress which continually rode up my thighs, and Mary-Ann, howling with laughter. Cary, embarrassed, pulled my dress down several times and, finally tired of us, good-naturedly put us onto the bus. We had to get home by ourselves, stinking drunk though we were. At the Bay, downtown, we impishly stole chocolate bars and managed to catch the No. 1 bus home. Mary-Ann and I sat up on the top of the hill next to her house, still shrieking with laughter and trying our darndest to sober up. After a couple of hours, she felt okay to go home, and I walked the mile home alone.

I would experience a hundred similar situations throughout high school and beyond, and drinking would become a way of life for me. Parties, drinking and hanging out with the older guys. Another escape.

Two weeks later, the group of us were again at Cary's brother's apartment. This time, Cary had the key and we had no trouble getting in. We drank a few beers and Cary's older brother Chris arrived. Feeling a little high, I ended up recklessly necking passionately with Chris in the bedroom. Tall, slim and blond, I was attracted to him immediately and felt excitement at his attraction to me. *No one had ever paid attention to me like this before.* Chris urged me to have sex with him, but having been raised with a strict Catholic upbringing, I said no. Little did he know I was a virgin and totally inexperienced with men. Luckily, it went no further than that, and Mary-Ann and I left for home.

The next day was Sunday, and, as usual, Mary-Ann and I walked around downtown. Unexpectedly, we ran into Chris walking out of Havana's Pizza—a cozy, little restaurant where he worked. Surprised to see us, he jovially asked us in for cokes and, to my surprise, asked me out on a date.

I met Chris downtown the following day and walked with him in the rain to Havana's. Steve, a friend of Chris's, was there at Havana's and encouraged me to phone Mary-Ann to join us.

Shortly before Mary-Ann's arrival, Chris and I sat talking and he asked me if I had ever dropped acid. I had no idea what he was talking about. He told me it would make me feel good. He was a little worried that I had never done drugs before, so he carefully broke the tablet of pure white lightening acid into two and gave me half the tab. Wanting to please him, this incredibly handsome fellow who was paying so much attention to me, I nervously made my way to the ladies' room and stared in awe at the tiny half tab of acid, feeling very unnerved. *This man had just given me drugs.* Feeling apprehensive about taking the full half tab, with careful precision I cautiously broke the tablet in half yet again and hurriedly gulped it, carefully placing the remaining quarter tab in my jacket pocket.

I emerged from the bathroom, wondering what the hell I had just done. I had absolutely no idea. No idea at all. Nor would I realize the devastating effect it would have on my life.

Within the hour, I began to feel very strange. My mouth was bone dry, and my eyes were glued wide open. I felt panicky at the powerful, strange sensation the acid was having on my mind and body and heaved a heavy sigh of relief when Mary-Ann finally walked through the door. I took her aside and quietly told her what I had done. She reacted with shock.

The potent drug took hold of me, and the four of us left the restaurant. It didn't take long before I was overpoweringly stoned and unable to comprehend what was happening around me. It was as if I were in a dream, floating. As we walked around downtown, I could not feel my body, nor could I feel my feet touch the ground. I could hear glitches of conversation, as if from a far-off planet, and Mary-Ann asking Chris if I was okay. He was obviously used to this thing that he called being *stoned*, but to me it was overwhelming. There was something thrilling yet incredibly bewildering about it—feeling out of my very existence—virtually out of my very mind. It was the most powerful and intoxicating experience I would ever know.

The four of us went to see the movie *Woodstock*, but I was too stoned to see the screen and too wrecked to realize I needed to put on my glasses to be able to see. Wildly hallucinating, the red licorice handed to me looked more like a cigarette. I stared at it, bewildered, unable to recognize it as something I could actually eat. Thankfully, I started to come down somewhat from the high of the drug when the movie ended and it was time to go home. Mary-Ann and I got on the bus and left Chris and Steve downtown. Her stop was before mine, and I was left behind to get off the bus by myself. I was nervous and paranoid on the bus, worried I would miss my stop. The stone from the acid had not yet worn off and I was still hallucinating. It was still pouring rain when I managed to clumsily grope my way to the exit door and stumble off the bus. I had difficulty walking and faltered down the back alley towards my house a block away. Peering skywards, I felt cool drops of rain splash on my face and stood there, entranced, enjoying the tingling wetness against my flushed skin. Suddenly, something struck me. I remembered and curiously felt in the pocket lining of my jacket. Sure enough, it was still there—the quarter tab of acid. This had not been a dream after all. Holding it carefully between my fingers, I peered at it wonderingly, this incredibly powerful little bit of compressed white powder, and reflected on the unbelievable effect it had had on me that evening. To my horror, the tiny bit of potent drug accidentally slipped through my fingers and dropped to the gravel at my feet. In desperation, I plunged to my knees in the pouring rain and frantically searched the ground for it. The rain, splashing hard against the small stones, dissolved it instantly. For several seconds I searched in vain. In those few moments I knew I was hooked on this acid shit. It took me away from my pain. It took me to a world outside of myself. I had found yet another escape.

I would drop LSD dozens more times throughout high school. It was a miracle that I survived it at all.

When I finally stepped inside the door at home, I was soaking wet and trembling like a leaf. Mother wouldn't stop yelling at me because I was late (it was only 8 p.m.) and demanded to know what was wrong with my eyes. I was still stoned, as was evidenced by my enormous pupils, dilated from the drug, and black as the night. She forbid me to see Chris again and Mary-Ann and I were both grounded the next day and forbidden to see or speak to each other. Silly. Two days later I saw my good friend and things were back to normal.

Surely, they knew they couldn't keep us apart.

Mary-Ann and I continued fighting with our mothers. I no longer cared about anything anymore, except getting out of the house and partying. I felt no sense of belonging, closeness or connection to home, so I would search for it elsewhere.

Occasionally I slept over at my friend Sandy's, and we would wait patiently until all was quiet in the house and cautiously sneak out, hitch-hike late at night, find a party, get stoned and party till dawn. Of course, we had to sneak back in, usually by 4:30 a.m. Surprisingly, her mother never caught us in any of our escapades. At other times Sandy would sneak out, arrive at my house promptly at midnight and throw tiny pebbles at my windowpane to wake me up. I would be fully clothed under the blankets and ready to go. Careful not to wake my younger sister Joan sleeping soundly beside me, I would quietly and stealthily climb out the window and down a ladder that I had carefully placed there for that purpose and the two of us would scamper off into the night to find whatever party was happening.

On one particular night I came home outrageously drunk, only to find the ladder had disappeared. Amazingly, mother let me into the house, insisting I was on drugs. Drunk as I was, I repeatedly vomited out my bedroom window again and again. The room stank like a brewery. I could hear yelling as the entire household was disrupted from sleep and poor Joan was ushered off to sleep elsewhere. The police arrived at 2 a.m., crudely woke me up and gave me one hell of a lecture. I really didn't give a shit. They eventually left, and I continued throwing up out the window throughout the night and into the early morning. Finally, exhausted and spent after hours of heaving, I succumbed to a drunken unconsciousness. The following day the detectives were back to interrogate me and told my mother they would investigate. Mom ordered me to hose the mess off the wall, which just made me retch all over again. I stayed miserably sick and painfully hung over for the next three days.

Winter had set in and it was bitterly cold outside. At Mom's refusal to allow me out of the house one particular night, I snuck out again, this time through the basement window. After several hours of partying, I came home, only to find the little piece of wood I had carefully jammed between the window and frame to keep it slightly ajar, gone. I was locked out and the temperature had dropped to a freezing -30°F. Damn. I banged on the front door again and again, but Mom refused to let me in. Undeterred, I crawled into the back of the old station wagon and huddled under a couple of thin, old blankets in a futile attempt to keep warm. As time went on, my body began to slowly freeze. I was numb and chilled to the bone. There was no longer any feeling in my hands or feet, and my heart rate slowed. I heard the front door open and my sisters crying and begging Mom to let me come in—that I would surely freeze to death out there. I didn't care. If she wanted me to freeze, that was fine with me. She'd have a hell of a time explaining to the authorities about her dead daughter's frozen body out there in the old station wagon.

An hour and a half later, she finally let me back in. I was grateful to feel the warmth of the house. Frozen solid as a block of ice, I slowly made my way downstairs to my bedroom and was surprised to see that my mattress was gone. She had taken it away. It didn't matter—I had warmth. I lay on the old, rusty iron springs, violently shaking and shivering. The thin blankets covering me did nothing to warm my frozen body, and I was worried that I could no longer feel my hands or feet. All night I shook. It wasn't until late the next morning that I was able to feel warmth. It was truly amazing that I didn't freeze to death that night. Too bad. Perhaps she would have been happier if I had. I lay with great discomfort on the rusty, old iron springs for the next three nights, but I never complained. Then she gave me my mattress back.

The drinking, partying and drugs continued. I was hopelessly out of control—we all were. But I didn't care. There was nothing left to care about.

Well, not quite. I still cared about my friends. One, in particular, I remember well. His name was Mike, and when I came close to overdosing on acid, hash and liquor, he was there to talk me down, reassuring me that I would be okay, that I could handle it. He was also one of the group. There came a time when he was strung out on heroin and was recovering in the psychiatric unit of the Foothills Hospital. On the few occasions I visited him in the hospital to comfort him, I would never have imagined that in 25 years, I myself would end up in the same psychiatric unit, albeit for a shockingly different reason.

My drug-taking got worse, and mother finally recognized that something was terribly wrong with the family and brought us in for family counseling. My brothers had all left home by now, as had Deirdre. So the five of us girls went for the first counseling session.

There were two psychologists in the room. Incredibly, they didn't focus on me and my drug-taking as I had presumed they would, but rather they focused on my mother. They asked her questions about her life—how she had met my father, and so on. For the first time in my life, I heard my mother speak about herself and about my long-dead father. I watched her weep in excruciating pain as she related something about having first met him in a post office in Saskatchewan, where the Royal Air Force had stationed him as a young man. It was both distressing and shocking to finally hear her talk about herself as a young girl and about my long-dead father after so many years had gone by. I sat there listening to her, all the while feeling my distress escalating. We all ended up tearful at the end of the session, but I was infuriated and silently enraged with her. She had never spoken of herself or my dead father before, and I didn't want to hear it now. It was just too excruciatingly painful. Too little, too late. I needed to hear all of this when I was a child, not now, at nearly seventeen years of age.

After two or three increasingly painful sessions, I refused to go back for further family counseling. As far as I was concerned, it was my mother who needed counseling—not me. She was the one who had been stuck in her grief all those years, unable to properly bond with me, unable to speak intimately with me, unable to share her reality with me, unable to give me the love, nurturing, direction or stability that I so desperately needed. That was not my fault. I would learn later on in my life that I was not to blame for my family's dysfunction. I did not create the dysfunction, nor could I fix it—I was merely born into it. I came to know in my heart that it was my mother who desperately needed psychological counseling to help her deal with chronic, unresolved emotional pain. Her pain had to be resolved long before I or any of my siblings could ever be helped. No, I was not going back to that painful crap. It was her mess to sort out, not mine.

The psychologists warned my mother that either we all went for counseling, or there would be no counseling at all. I did not believe that bullshit for a moment and remained adamant. I would not go. It was obvious to me that they all saw my drug-taking as being the family's primary problem. What a load of crap. My drug-taking was a result of feeling emotional neglect far more deeply than the others. I would come to understand with incredible clarity years down the road that the child on drugs is most often the symptom-bearer of the family's problems and that much of what I did during that time in my life was not about me, but rather it was about what was done to me.

No, I was not going back. They could all go if they wanted to, but they would have to go without me. From that moment on, each member of my family held me culpable for the family's dysfunction and continued deterioration, and because of my refusal to go back to family counseling, each would, in their own way, blame me for the rest of their lives.

I became the Family Scapegoat.

3 The Beginning of the End

It was on June 9, 1970, towards the end of grade 10, at a night club called Apollo, that I first set eyes upon him. He was tall and immensely good-looking, with beautiful dark hair and thick, dark eyebrows, and I fell for him straightaway. I found out his name was Bill. He was in grade 12 and good friends with Cary and Gary. I was just sixteen at the time and felt an overpowering schoolgirl crush on Bill almost immediately.

Cary and Bill were best friends. Bill had obviously heard the story of Cary's older brother Chris getting me stoned on acid and candidly offered to get me a four-tab acid to "blow my mind." One-sixteenth of that amount rendered me incoherent and cataleptic, and I recoiled to think what irreparable brain damage four tabs of acid would do. Surely, I would end up in a vegetative state, locked in a mental institution for the remainder of my life. No, I would not dream of doing such a foolish thing. Surely, Bill was joking.

Bill glibly suggested that if I ever wanted to buy drugs, he could get me whatever I wanted, and true to his word, I was able to purchase psilocybin, mescaline and MDA from him. I was curious to know where the drugs came from—was there someone cooking up a new batch of mescaline or LSD in a laboratory night after night? And who came up with those silly names—Yellow Sunshine, Red Spec, Pink Smear, Green Pent and Strawberry Barrel? It really didn't matter what the drugs were or where they came from; what mattered was that I had easy access to them.

Dances were held at the school, and I would inevitably run into Bill. He did not have a girlfriend at the time and frequently asked me to dance. I loved dancing with Bill—he took my breath away. I was ecstatic when he finally asked me out on a date to the movies. We never made it to the movies, however, and, as usual, ended up passionately groping each other's bodies for hours. We never actually slept together, although he urgently wanted me to. I loved the beautiful feel of his body pressed tightly to mine, but I wanted more than sex from Bill, and I believe he sensed it. I needed love and attention and intimacy, and he only wanted sex, so I quickly learned to settle for just being with him in a very sensuous way and accepted what little emotional involvement he was willing to give.

Bill was in grade 12 for the third time. He stayed half the semester, managed to obtain all of his credits and left high school for good. The rest of the group had already finished and left. Some had been kicked out, others had dropped out of school. I missed the group we had—the camaraderie we had all shared, the lunches in the cafeteria and the walks to the river. I felt an overwhelming loneliness and dejection after they had all left.

It was my final year at high school. I was startled to see Bill back at the school, but this time he was not alone. He was arm in arm with Darlene, his girlfriend. I felt a strange sadness seeing the two of them together. I was not jealous that he had found someone, but rather I felt very disheartened, for I had indeed adored him. As he sauntered down the hall in that alluring way of his, he passed me briefly and I stared at him in wonder, marveling at his good looks. *A child with Bill would be beautiful—so beautiful indeed, I thought to myself.* How utterly foolish of me. Such a thing would never happen. I had always sensed I was not good enough for Bill.

I was confused as to what Bill saw in Darlene. She was aggressive and overly controlling, and it was impossible to get anywhere near Bill with her hanging on his arm. Nor was she a beautiful woman, and Bill was the most handsome man I had ever met.

Three months previous, a friend of mine, Cecilia, had brought me to a place everyone called *810*—an old, unkempt Victorian-style house on the outskirts of downtown. The walls were painted black as night, with bits of white resembling stars. Cecilia introduced me to a fellow slouched in an old armchair. His name was Ernest. Certainly, he was not much to look at—he was skinny and scrawny, with dirty-blond, scraggly hair and a quick laugh. And no wonder. Cecilia informed me he made a living selling drugs.

He scrutinized me lasciviously. I was a pretty, young girl with an unmistakably slim, attractive figure and shoulder-length brown hair and brown eyes. I caught the unmistakable leer on Ernest's face as he took sharp note of my shapely legs and short skirt, and I felt an immediate revulsion towards this creepy, little man.

A few days later I visited *810* again with Cecilia on a break from school. An air of excitement permeated throughout the old house, and we watched with curiosity as a package that had just arrived was carefully opened in front of us. Scrupulously wrapped in several layers of plastic and paper was a large, one-inch thick slab of black hash. I had never seen so much dope in my entire life. Ernest and John sat down to cut the slab into grams. They were having a great time laughing at how much money they were going to make selling it. A weigh scale was nearby as well as foil for wrapping the grams. I felt an incredible uneasiness at the drug activity that was obviously going on at *810*.

Teasingly, Cecilia told Ernest that I was untouched and a virgin, and he immediately began pursuing me. Believing I wasn't good enough for anyone else except Ernest [*I certainly wasn't good enough for Bill—he had found someone else*], I finally gave in and dated him. He purchased gifts and spent money on me in an attempt to seduce me, and he continually pressured me for sex. Finally, I decided to play it safe in case something did happen and got a prescription for birth control pills and hid it in my bedroom where no one could find it.

A few days later I walked into my room unsuspectingly to find my mother searching my room. She held my diary in one hand and her other hand clenched a piece of paper. She had found my prescription.

"What's this?" she yelled.

I stood silent and lowered my gaze to the floor so as not to look at this irrational, crazed woman screaming at me.

"You're a slut! You're nothing but a slut!"

She spat the shameful words at me and tore the piece of paper to shreds. *There goes my prescription, I thought with dismay.* She threw the diary on the bed and abruptly left, slamming the door behind her. I didn't understand the horrible shame she had just dumped on me. She had unloaded shame on me my entire life, particularly sexual shame. I truly thought I was doing the responsible thing, getting that birth control prescription. I certainly couldn't go back to the doctor for another one [*he had shamed me as well for even asking for it*], so I had no protection and no way of knowing what was about to happen.

It was close to my eighteenth birthday, and Ernest took me out for drinks to the Highlander Hotel. It was a very popular drinking bar, a place where all the in-crowd hung out. We sat at a table, and, as usual, Ernest pulled out a bulky wad of money and ordered several pitchers of draught beer. His friends joined us and before the drinking began, I excused myself to use the ladies' room. On the way back to the table, I passed the door to the entrance and was startled to see Bill standing there. *Oh God, he was alone.*

He smiled that beautiful, charming smile of his, and I smiled back. I still adored Bill, and it felt comforting to see him again.

"Come on—let's go," he said.

Without hesitation, I answered, "Sure."

He didn't have to ask me twice. I left the bar with Bill and deserted Ernest back at the table. He would be fine. He had his friends to drink with. I didn't care. I wanted to be with Bill. That's all I ever wanted—to be with Bill.

We took a taxi to Rick's apartment, a friend of Bill's. Bill had the key and let us in. It was empty. In no time at all, we were in the bedroom, completely naked. I had never been naked with a man before, and if I were to choose one to be naked with, this was the man. Once again we were together, and I felt wonderfully contented, lying in his arms. Our impassioned bodies were ripe with lust; I loved being sexual with him and he with me. Incredibly, we were both straight and stone-cold sober, which made the passion all the more beautiful and intense.

He wanted to have sex with me, but I kept saying no. He tried fervently, pushing his penis up between my legs again and again. I wouldn't let him enter. So he continued pushing, in an attempt to penetrate. As much as I longed to have sex with Bill, I couldn't let it happen. I was still a virgin.

The door opened unexpectedly, and the blinding light from the living room starkly illuminated us, exposing our nudity. Bill yelped in surprise, jumped up and hurried to the door while I scrambled for the sheet to cover my nakedness. I could hear muffled voices as Bill spoke in a hushed tone to whoever was there. Then the door closed quietly and Bill came back to me. But it was over. The passion had been diffused. We both dressed hurriedly and left the apartment. I went home alone by cab.

Bill went back to Darlene; I went back to Ernest.

Three weeks passed and I began to feel uneasy. Was my period late? Bill had not penetrated me, nor had he ejaculated. I couldn't possibly be pregnant. I knew it was just a fantasy—to have Bill's child. So I must be late again. That happened sometimes.

Ernest took me out drinking again. Feeling despondent, I drank profusely, to the point of near unconsciousness. Ernest brought me back to *810* and put me in Steve's bed downstairs—a makeshift mattress and sheets on the floor, with a black sheet draped across the open doorway. The room was spinning around me as Ernest stripped my clothes off and crudely climbed on top of me. On the verge of passing out, I was too drunk to fight him off or push him away, and obviously taking that as consent, he selfishly and crassly took my virginity. It was painful, and I did not enjoy what he was doing to me. His body fluids were all over me, the scent of his sex hung heavily in the air and I felt repulsed and wanted to vomit. When it was over he got up, and I could hear him in the next room speaking quietly to someone on the telephone telling that person that it was over—that he had just had sex with me. It was obvious he had just dumped some poor girl. Guilt-ridden and feeling overwhelming shame at what he had done to me, I blacked out and sank into unconsciousness.

The next morning very little mention was made of the previous night. Steve yelled at Ernest about the blood on the sheets, and Ernest sheepishly told him he would clean them. I walked with Ernest outside and stood leaning against the fence at the front of the yard. It had snowed during the night and the air was cold. I stood there shivering in a thin jacket, miserably hung over and nauseated, desperately wanting a hot shower to wash away the ugliness of the previous night. Ernest seemed pleased with himself—*well why not, he had just scored a virgin*, but I felt dirty, unclean and violated. Gloomily, I thought to myself: *Well, if I wasn't pregnant by Bill, I sure as hell am now.*

And I was right. Ernest had indeed gotten me pregnant.

I deeply regretted that it had not been Bill, the man I had adored throughout high school. My heart felt so heavy with disappointment. Why did the first time have to be so nauseating, so repulsive, so unpleasant? Why did it have to be with someone I felt very little attraction towards—certainly not a sexual attraction? And why did this objectionable, little man have to climb on top of me, taking advantage of me in my obvious state of drunkenness, knowing full well I was still a virgin? Everyone would say I deserved it—after all, I was drunk, I was at his place late at night and I had dressed sensually, setting everything in motion. It was all my fault. Certainly, that was what everyone would say. *She asked for it. She got what she deserved.*

Two months passed and I still hadn't had my period. Concerned, I told Ernest. It was obvious he didn't want a child. He hadn't used any kind of protection himself that night, and he knew he was the father. At seventeen years of age, the unexpected pregnancy traumatized me, and I couldn't help feeling a demoralizing shame that all of this had happened to me.

It was still early in my pregnancy, and Ernest gave me the name of an abortion doctor. Nervously, I made an appointment. The doctor shocked and distressed me with his harsh, cruel words. "You realize if this child is born alive, I have to kill it, and you're the murderer."

Appalled and terrified to hear such ugly words spat at me, I fled from his office and never returned. I wasn't prepared to be labeled a murderer.

The weeks relentlessly slipped by, time was running out and I finally succumbed to Ernest's pressure to see another abortion doctor.

To my surprise, he was a wonderful, decent man. He was kind and gentle with me and calmly told me that an abortion procedure was far too risky at this late date and to forget about it. He told me that I was further along in my pregnancy than I thought. There was something very disquieting about his words, but I was too traumatized and confused to fully comprehend what he was saying. He comforted me and gently informed me that I was going to have a healthy, happy baby, and for the first time in my pregnancy, I no longer felt ashamed.

Finally, I had to tell mother. To my surprise, she was deathly quiet. Was that because she had torn up my prescription for birth control pills? Or was there something else? Her silence troubled me. I didn't blame her for anything and I knew it was my fault. *You made your bed—now you sleep in it.*

School was finally over, I moved away from home and into the place called *810*. I could not possibly go through the pregnancy in front of my mother. I would have been very uncomfortable doing so, and although she asked me to stay at home, she didn't argue when I left.

The drug dealing continued at *810*, and I grew increasingly unhappy and despondent with what was going on at the house. There was no refrigerator to keep milk fresh or food from spoiling. Mother had been strict with Ernest and told him that I needed lots of milk and plenty of fresh fruits and vegetables. That was impossible without a fridge. The filthiness of *810* discouraged me, and even in an advanced stage of pregnancy, I got down on my hands and knees and scrubbed the dirt and grime from the kitchen floor and counters. I only wanted the place to be clean and look nice. My efforts were in vain.

Low-life drug people continuously trampled through the house, bought drugs, smoked up and partied from morning till night. The bathroom was always dirty and soiled from all the guys using it, and the rest of the house was in a constant state of disarray. No one bothered to clean anything. Disheartened by the state of chaos, I begged Ernest repeatedly to move out with me. He seemed happy to stay put and saw nothing wrong with *810*, but I persisted, and he grudgingly agreed. When September arrived, Ernest, Steve and I moved into a basement suite in Bowness.

I was seven months pregnant when the phone call came. It was Mary-Ann. I was delighted to hear from my best friend once again. She was getting married in a couple of months and told me her sister would be her maid of honour at her wedding instead of me. *Oh God. We had always planned that I would be her maid of honour.* Deeply hurt, I managed to hide the disappointment in my voice and told Mary-Ann I didn't mind being her bridesmaid instead. There was a long pause. I wondered if something was wrong. *No, you can't be my bridesmaid either.* Silence. Dead silence.

Oh God, she was ashamed of me.

She was explaining something about her parents insisting it be that way, but I could no longer hear her. Somehow, I managed to tell her that I was okay with her change of plans and hastily got off the phone. Reeling, I staggered down the hallway to the bedroom, clutching my protruding belly, and fell on the bed, heartbroken. I wept unceasingly for hours. So inexorably profound was my sobbing, I was terrified I would miscarry. My best friend was ashamed of me and so were her parents. I was inconsolable that night and for several nights after that.

I waited patiently for my invitation to Mary-Ann's wedding to arrive in the mail. It never came. I had not been invited to my best friend's wedding.

I could never forgive Mary-Ann for what she had done, so I tried to forget.

It was a cold, wintry October morning when the day finally arrived. I awoke with unusual pains at 6 a.m. and nudged Ernest from sleep. He was angry at me for awakening him so early.

"The baby isn't due for another three weeks!" he scolded me. "If you didn't drink so much, you wouldn't be having false labour pains."

Disgruntled and annoyed at me for disturbing his sleep, he grumpily rolled over and in seconds was again fast asleep. Noiselessly I got up, not wanting to disturb him further. He could be so miserable. I had not been drinking and was hurt by his nasty remark. This strange pain was not my imagination. He was right, however, about the baby not being due for at least another three weeks.

My feet padded softly on the carpet as I tip-toed down the dim hallway to the bathroom. Quietly, I closed the door and turned on the light. A warm glow radiated heat in the small room. Turning on the facets, I ran a scalding hot bath and carefully lowered myself into the steaming water. I lay there contentedly, luxuriating in the heat, my round belly swelling with the impending birth. My back had been bothering me for several weeks with the extra weight I had been carrying. The hot water seemed to wash away the pain and it felt so wonderfully soothing. Lulled by the steam swirling and curling towards the ceiling, I felt a drowsiness overcome me, and my eyelids fluttered shut.

I drifted in and out of slumber, comforted by the steaming, hot water. I thought of the imminent birth of the baby and reflected on my disquieting decision to give the baby up for adoption. All of this was so very painful and confusing. I had been so appallingly drunk the night Ernest had selfishly taken my virginity and I had become pregnant. He never wanted a child. And I wanted Ernest. Or so I thought. I had so many misgivings about this selfish, homely, little man whose only concern was money. Money and selling drugs.

How was I going to handle such an overwhelming responsibility at eighteen years of age? I could not do it alone, and I knew I could not count on Ernest to be there for me or the baby. I was too young. My doubts plagued me with an excruciating inner torment.

The water had become tepid and I jerked wide awake.

I stood up slowly, gasped and doubled over in pain, clutching my belly. Knowing I was about to pass out, I groped awkwardly for something to support me as the room spun around. I managed to steady myself and stumbled out of the bathtub. Fumbling for a bathrobe, I clumsily groped my way down the hall to the kitchen, nervously switching on lights as I went.

I put water on for tea, sat down at the kitchen table and tried to calm myself. The room was warm, and I felt comfortable after such a luxurious, hot bath. The clock on the wall ticked softly and I sat there, peacefully gazing at the snow flurries whirling past the kitchen window. It was still early and dark outside. I watched as the minute hand of the clock rhythmically ticked away the seconds. Another pain. *I wished I hadn't missed my last doctor's appointment. Damn.* I had been so traumatized by the pregnancy, I had not read anything about childbirth and was regretting that now.

The kettle whistled and I got up and poured a cup of tea and sat back down. Over an hour went by. *Why weren't the pains going away? There seemed to be more of them coming.* I continued to watch the clock and poured another cup of tea. Surely, they would disappear soon, and I could go back to a warm, cozy bed on this miserably cold winter morning. *Oh God, another sharp pain.*

My eyes were transfixed on the clock as the realization hit me, hard. The pains were coming precisely every minute and a half. *How could that be?* Anxiously, I got up from the table to reach for the telephone on the counter.

"Mom, it's me. I'm having these pains."

The alarm was unmistakable in my mother's voice when I related the timing of the contractions. "Get to the hospital fast! I'll call your doctor! Just go!"

Oh God, this was it! And I had wasted so much time with the bath and all! Frightened, I hastened back to the bedroom and shook Ernest from sleep once more. He was livid that I had awakened him a second time.

"Fine! I'll take you to the damn hospital, but I'm not going without a shower!"

Angrily, he threw off the blankets and stomped down the hallway to the bathroom. I heard the sound of the shower running and nervously dressed. I sat trembling on the edge of the bed, clutching a brown paper bag with a nightgown and toothbrush thrown hastily inside. Terribly confused, I couldn't think of anything else to bring with me to the hospital. I was not prepared. Not prepared at all. This was not supposed to happen for at least another three weeks.

The contractions were coming faster and becoming increasingly more powerful. I could barely breathe, and my heart pounded furiously. *Oh God, I'm not going to make it to the hospital! I thought in alarm.* The sound of a razor tapping against the sink filled me with further alarm and dismay. *Oh God, no! Now he was shaving!*

In full distress, I was unable to move from the edge of the bed. After what seemed an eternity, he finally appeared in the doorway. He gaped at me, realizing his mistake. There was a rush for the car.

It was still dark outside, and snow still swirled about.

We arrived at the hospital at 8:40 a.m.

Twenty minutes later, at 9 a.m. on a cold and wintry October morning, my beautiful son was born. The nurse gently placed him in a clear bassinet next to me, and I stared wonderingly at this beautiful, little thing with dark hair. *This was my son! How incredibly lovely he was!* And such a brave, little soul—he hadn't cried through the birth at all.

I heard the nurse's sheepish voice.

"Oh! You're not keeping this baby, are you?" In a broken hearted voice, I managed to whisper:

"No—no, I'm not." Ernest must have told them downstairs. The nurse mumbled an embarrassed apology and whisked the beautiful infant away. I was filled with an incredible, aching emptiness as I watched him leave the room. I just wanted to hold him. I lay there— isolated, alone and numb with shock. No one bothered to speak to me, and the room quickly emptied. Tears welled up in my eyes, and I was relieved when they finally wheeled me from the delivery room.

The next five days were straight from hell.

A woman from the Department of Social Services met Ernest and I in the hospital cafeteria. There was a wonderful couple who wanted to adopt the baby, and she had the documents ready for me to sign. Nervously, I held the pen just above the line to sign my name, but for the life of me, I could not force my hand to write. I simply couldn't sign my name. The woman came back, undeterred, day after day.

Night after night, I was plagued with dreams of a dark-haired, little boy, pulling at my skirt and stubbornly following me around, pleading to know why I had given him away. I would awaken gasping for air, soaking wet and delirious, a paralyzing scream stuck in my throat. The pain was unbearable. Emotionally, I was dying.

Ernest was there every day with empty promises of marriage and security if I kept the baby. I knew he only wanted to save face in front of his family and friends. I had no job and no money, and I couldn't possibly ask anyone for help. This was my responsibility. I had gotten myself into this mess, and I had to figure it out alone.

There were three other mothers in the room who had given birth, and several times a day the room filled with nursing infants. I pulled the curtains around my bed and crawled under the covers, my body contorted with agonizing sobs. After a while, I recognized the times the infants were coming and quickly retreated down the hallway to a quiet place to hide and weep silently.

Finally, the fifth day arrived and it was time to go home. The other mothers had all left the hospital with their babies, and I was the last to leave. For thirty minutes I was alone in the room and sat on the bed in the blissful, peaceful silence.

The nurse came in, glanced at me and asked if there was anything she could get me before I left the hospital. I stared at her and answered:

"Yes. I came here with something, and I'm going to leave here with something. Go get me my baby."

The nurse's mouth dropped open and she stood there, transfixed.

"Now!" I commanded her.

She gaped at me, stumbled and left the room. I sat there, amazed at what I had just done. The nurse returned a few minutes later with the baby and gave him to me. I held him in my arms for the first time. He was beautiful, my little son. I could never have left the hospital without him. I stared at him in wonder and amazement. My beautiful, beautiful, little son.

The nurse went over his feeding schedule and gave me some bottles and booklets. There wasn't much time to brief me on caring for him before it was time to go.

I left the hospital with my son and never looked back.

Holding my beautiful child, I thought about my father. I knew very little about him. Mother never spoke of him or her life with him in Ireland before coming to Canada. Her inability to speak left us yearning for a history, a past, an identity. I did know he was from Belfast, Northern Ireland, and his father, William, my grandfather, was a seaman from County Tyrone. She never spoke of my grandparents, and I discovered many years later from an Irish cousin that my grandfather, William Lyttle, lived with a woman named Mary Ellen Savage (McKeown) and had sons by her, one of whom was my father. Years later, I sent away to Belfast for my father's service record, knowing he had been in the Royal Air Force, and was surprised to discover that he had been an aircraft engineer. I never knew that. It was really the only information I could obtain about him. It really didn't matter. He didn't exist. He had been forgotten.

I named my son Joseph, after my father.

4 *The Dance*

I adapted to motherhood and little Joseph over the next several months. It was difficult at first, getting up at all hours of the night, but I learned to adjust to little Joseph's day schedule, sleeping when he slept, getting up when he got up. Gradually, I got the hang of it. He was such a darling, little baby, never colicky, but always smiling and laughing. He gave me such pleasure.

Ernest, however, was a different story. He proved to be a master of deception. The promises of marriage and security he made to me in the hospital never materialized. Foolishly, I made up a wedding invitation list, but Ernest refused to commit to a wedding date. Marriage was not forthcoming and never would be. I was devastated to have been so deceived by him. After only six months, my expectations were completely dashed, and recognizing the hopelessness of the situation and having nowhere else to go, I moved in with a girlfriend on 29th Avenue in the southwest quadrant of the city.

Ernest was perturbed by my sudden departure with the baby and pressured me to return. My abrupt withdrawal from him took him by surprise and triggered his own abandonment fears, and he used seduction in an attempt to win me back. I gave in to his persuasions and slept with him. I knew it was inappropriate and deeply regretted it. I do not believe he actually wanted me back, but rather he felt guilty about his son's absence.

The dance had begun.

Two weeks passed and I began experiencing severe abdominal pains. Continually doubled over with severe cramping and bleeding, I had difficulty standing for any length of time. I told Ernest about the pain, and he casually said it would probably go away if I lay down. It didn't—the pain got worse. I was having trouble running after little Joseph and continually needed to rest. It occurred to me that Ernest was somewhat nervous about the obvious worsening of my condition, and finally, one night to my surprise, he reluctantly came by to speak to me.

I had VD. Ernest explained he had been with a hooker, contracted the disease through her and passed it along to me through intercourse the last time we had been together. He told me he had gotten rid of it, and I should too. *Bastard! And I had been in such severe pain for weeks.* Torn by his betrayal, but too ill to argue, I accompanied him to a grungy-looking STD clinic. Prostitutes and vulgar-looking street people sauntered through the clinic; their appearances both alarmed and infuriated me. *No one at this clinic was going to touch or treat me—I didn't belong here.* I felt bitter resentment at having to suffer such a shameful indignity, refused to see anyone at the clinic and angrily told Ernest to take me home. He obliged. I went back to my wonderful doctor and he asked me where on earth did I manage to pick up a dose of chlamydia. *My boyfriend gave it to me.* He was kind and gentle as usual and told me to be careful—chlamydia causes sterilization, if left untreated. I was stunned. *Wonderful—perhaps Ernest left me sterile.*

Ernest apologized profusely and promised it would never happen again.

Several weeks passed and I struggled not only with the enormity of what Ernest had done to me, but also if I was better off without him. But it was not to be. I did not have the strength, wisdom or self-esteem to realize that going back to Ernest was the biggest mistake I could have made. I simply did not have the courage to stay away. By now I had indeed become addicted to the relationship, accustomed to the abuse and bonded to the trauma. I had learned to live with intolerable abuse and trauma growing up, and this was not that much different. It was, at least, familiar to me.

It's possible there may have been a small part of Ernest that actually wanted his child, but he definitely did not want the responsibility or the commitment, nor did he want me. A man will tell you who he is and what he wants, but I wasn't listening. Ernest had told me he never wanted a child or marriage or responsibility. I never listened.

We moved into a duplex on 68th Avenue. It was a disaster from the beginning. There was constant fighting, and Ernest repeatedly took off to party, drink and smoke up with the two fellows who lived in the other half of the duplex, leaving me alone with the baby. Gradually, the little one and I learned to cling to each other. We were all each of us had. I loved little Joseph and would never have abandoned him. And little Joseph loved me. Ernest desperately wanted his freedom, and I wanted him to commit. He wanted the drug life back, and I wanted a quiet, stable family life.

Joseph was just eight months old, and it was time for his baptism. Having been brought up in a strict Catholic family, I knew my mother wanted him baptized. I'm not sure what I wanted. We drove to my mother's house the night before the baptism to meet Father Lough. He was a young priest and asked us a lot of questions. *Are you going to bring the child up in the Catholic church?*, etc. I answered yes, of course I was going to raise him in the Catholic church. More questions. The evening wore on. Mom had made lovely sandwiches and desserts, and I thought the meeting went well. When it was over, the three of us left for home.

The next day Ernest, the baby and I, dressed in our Sunday best, sat proudly in the front pew of the church along with the godparents, with my family directly behind us. Father Lough got up in the pulpit. His words cut into me like a knife.

"As you all know, I should not be here performing this baptism, and you all know why."

God, no! He was referring to me—the woman living in sin in the front row. He was humiliating me in front of everyone. I bowed my head in horrific shame. Someone snickered. I wanted to run with the baby, screaming out the church door, but I couldn't move. Mercilessly, he continued:

"I have spoken with my elders, and they have allowed me to go ahead with this baptism. I want you all to know, however, that it is against my better judgment. But since you are all here, I will go ahead with it anyway."

The bastard! This was a priest? What a God-awful shame! I couldn't hear any more words coming from his mouth. I had brought a beautiful, sweet, innocent child of God to him to be baptized, and he not only stood in judgment of me, but also shamed me in the cruelest way imaginable. Mortified to death, I prayed the earth would open up and swallow me whole. My face burnt beet red with shame. That ugly shame. *I knew this shame well.*

But my son got baptized. I hated the sight of his baptismal certificate, and the special baptism candles given to me as a memento of his great day were shamefully hidden away and never looked upon again. It was a day I wanted only to forget.

It would be years before I stepped foot inside a church again. I simply didn't believe in it anymore.

The fighting with Ernest continued and became horrendous. This time, the relationship had lasted only two months.

I moved out again. I went back to 29th Avenue, but this time moved into a small apartment in a four-unit older house. I was familiar with the area, and I tried desperately to heal my broken spirit. I was left unbearably traumatized and scarred by the abusive, toxic relationship with Ernest and couldn't seem to heal. I felt so abandoned and so terrifyingly alone. At night, panic and terror gripped me at being so isolated with the baby in that drafty, creaky old house. I often heard heavy footsteps directly outside my door late at night, and I continually imagined someone was coming to break in and kill me. The gruesome thoughts would not leave me, and I instinctively knew I was not at peace. Joseph often slept with me, and we clung to each other at night. Hearing his peaceful, rhythmic breathing next to me often quieted my terror and lulled me to sleep.

There was an outdoor swimming pool nearby, and I frequently took Joseph swimming with me. He loved the water, and I loved being with him. Giant poplar trees surrounded the pool, and a large, beautiful, grassy park enabled little Joey to run and play. It was a peaceful, quiet place, and I loved taking him there. Sometimes we enjoyed a picnic on the huge, grassy field. We spent the summer at the old house on 29th Avenue, but it was time to move again.

Ernest helped me search for another place, and we found one closer to downtown, on 15th Avenue.

Moving day arrived. I packed everything up and sat patiently waiting for Ernest to come and move me and the baby as he had promised. The day wore on and little Joey was getting cranky and restless. I unpacked food and milk for him. Ernest still hadn't made an appearance. I sat there all day surrounded by boxes and with baby, but with no one to help me move. It was getting dark and there was still no sign of him. Thankfully, friends of Ernest unexpectedly dropped by to say hello, and I begged them to help me move. They did. As we were leaving with the last of my stuff, Ernest showed up, drunk. He had been drinking with the girlfriend I used to live with, and he had been busy helping her paint her kitchen or some damn thing. He had forgotten about me and the baby. Of course. We never mattered to him. He probably slept with her. I was in tears and furious with him.

Little Joseph and I got settled in the apartment, alone.

One night, while getting little Joey off to bed, I noticed something crawling on the blankets. I tore the sheets off, and several caterpillar-like bugs scampered for cover. *Oh God, there were bugs in his bed!* They were all over. I banged at the bed to scare them away and tried to comfort Joey, telling him they were all gone. He was nearly a year old and afraid of the bugs and wouldn't get back into bed. I couldn't blame the little guy. *That's okay—you can sleep in Mommy's bed.* It became a ritual night after night. I pounded the heck out of his mattress to scare away the little creatures and hoped to God they didn't come back to bite him while he was sleeping. It gave real meaning to the old saying, *Night, night, sleep tight, don't let the bed bugs bite.*

Upon closer examination, I discovered the bugs had infiltrated the entire apartment. I felt a horrible revulsion at my discovery and complained to the landlord—a big, ugly, obnoxious man with fleshy nodules covering his face and neck. I often caught him leering at me whenever he saw me in the hallway. He was unsympathetic and emphatically denied there were any kind of bugs in the apartment. I reminded him that he had promised to shampoo the carpets and paint my apartment before I moved in and that he had not yet done so. He gruffly told me the place didn't need it and he didn't have the time. He only wanted my welfare voucher for rent.

Failing to convince the landlord he needed to call a bug exterminator, I telephoned the Department of Health myself. I trapped several bugs in a jar to provide evidence of their existence, and the Department of Health not only forced the landlord to paint my apartment, shampoo the carpets and spray for the silverfish, as they were called, but also told him to paint the hallways and shampoo the carpets throughout the building. The health inspector also directed him to spray for bugs on the first two floors of the apartment building. The landlord was furious that I had compelled him to spend money, and in retaliation, only one month after moving in, I was given three months' notice to vacate. He later kept my damage deposit and charged me for the bug spraying, painting and carpet cleaning. I was quickly learning what an ugly world it was.

Ernest's promises fell far short. I heard through friends that he planned on marrying me. I could not figure this man out.

He worked close by and often came over to my apartment for lunch. During those visits, he always discussed the rules that I would have to follow before we got back together. He was emphatic about this. He was free to go out with the boys two nights a week, and he could have lunch with his secretary whenever he wanted. I couldn't remember the other rules, nor did I care to. Nor could I understand why the rules were always drafted in his favour and never in mine. What about being a family and making time for his son, making time for me? Shouldn't we come first? I didn't understand the rules, and I had trouble accepting them. I remember Ernest's own mother telling Ernest on Joey's first birthday:

"You treat your dog better than you do your family."

I knew she was right. He did indeed. That dog of Ernest's got better treatment than we ever did.

Our relationship continued to fail miserably. Ernest only dropped by for lunch and to have sex, and although it felt sleazy, I let him have his way. I often felt inexplicably exasperated by the time he left the apartment. One day he would discuss getting married to me; the next day the marriage was off. Similarly, he would discuss living with me; the next day living together was out of the question. He tormented me with his unpredictable responses. Young and naive, I did not realize at the time it was severe emotional abuse, nor did I realize just how damaging his unpredictable responses were to me. It was Ernest's way of effectively keeping me on edge and off balance. I was hypervigilant and lived in fear, always expecting a change of mind, a change of heart. I was very unsettled and anxious, never knowing what to expect. Ernest was indeed very clever that way and knew how to abuse me emotionally. I was so young, so naive, so foolish, I learned to live with it. Hell, I bonded to it. I was addicted to him as well as the drama and chaos of our relationship, and I knew no other way to live.

The dance continued.

If I didn't hear from Ernest, the panic of abandonment gripped me, and feeling I was about to be deserted, in desperation I phoned him. Again and again he explicitly told me not to phone him. He was the one in control, and I had to obey the rules.

When he did invite me to his place for a party, he ignored me and leered and lusted after other women who were there. Fights inevitably ensued on the drive home, and he yelled at me that he didn't love me. I cried at his cruelty. He took a sickening pleasure in hurting me, constantly criticizing and reprimanding me. I knew in my heart that I was sick of him, sick of his deceit, sick of his lying, sick of his leering after other women and, more important, sick of his emotional unavailability. I often wished the relationship would just die.

But the relationship would not die. It had to run its course. The dance wasn't over yet, and the music was still playing.

There were a few times I did my own thing with friends or stayed at Mom's for a weekend. It was times like these, when I actually demonstrated some independence, that it would be Ernest's turn to feel the twinges of abandonment grip him, and he would then run after me. That was when he would tell me we were getting back together and actually bought me a diamond ring as bait and seducement. If I wasn't feeling abandoned, he was.

I had lived on welfare since Joey's birth nearly a year ago. I felt it was very important to bond with my son that first year and had always intended to return to work and had no intention of staying on welfare. Ernest said he would live with me if welfare paid for it, and that way he'd be living for free. It was then that I decided I would go back to work.

The day before Christmas, just four months after moving into the apartment with the bugs, I moved back in with Ernest.

Terrible things happened at Tregillus Street.

He took me to his firm's Christmas party at his employer's lovely home. As usual, he abandoned me at the party, and I began drinking heavily. I felt very self-conscious, surrounded by executive-type people I didn't know and didn't care to know. *I didn't belong here.* Ernest was having a great time talking it up to every female at the gathering, particularly his secretary. Several times I quietly approached him and told him I felt uncomfortable and uneasy with these people, in these fancy surroundings and implored him to take me home. He refused and told me he was having a good time and wasn't about to leave because of me. Ignoring me, he walked away and left me stranded. I did not have the money for a taxi home, and I felt apprehensive that something terrible was going to happen.

It did.

I stood at the top of the stairs leading to the lower party floor with a glass of rye in my hand, feeling very intoxicated and speaking with the boss's son. I asked him to hold my glass, and obligingly, he did. Rocking gently back and forth on the top step, I lost my balance and tumbled head over heels down the flight of stairs, landing with a thud at the bottom. *Surely, he'll take me home now! I thought ruefully.*

Several alarmed guests helped me up, and Ernest was summoned. I think he found it amusing that I had fallen down the stairs. Once again, I begged and pleaded with him to take me home. He was angry at me for asking yet again and insisted I was not going to spoil his good time. He refused to drive me home and once again deserted me to be with others at the party. So I continued drinking.

I was again at the top of the stairs, speaking to someone else this time. I asked the fellow, a complete stranger to me, if he wanted to watch me fall down the stairs. He chuckled, not realizing I was deadly serious. He gaped in alarm as I teetered on the top stair and fell convincingly backwards. This time, I effectively smashed into the beautiful glass cabinet directly across the landing from the foot of the stairs. My hand went through the beveled, ornate glass window, and I ended up in a crumpled heap on the marble floor. Glass from the cabinet shattered and fragments were strewn over the tiles around me, and the sensual blue dress I wore that evening was irreparably torn and stained with blood. I thought to myself with rueful satisfaction, *Now he has to take me home!*

And he did.

Guests were quietly shocked at what had happened. A deathly hush descended over the party and the music was turned down low. Everyone stared at me in disbelief and made a pathway for me to leave. Ernest was furious and embarrassed and apologized profusely to his employer and everyone else on the way out. He had to hold me up, drunk as I was. *Finally, I was going home. That's all I wanted. I just wanted to go home.*

He screamed at me all the way home. When we mercifully arrived at the house, Ernest announced he was leaving for good and refused to get out of the car. Fiercely intoxicated, I stumbled out of the car, grabbed a brick beside the house and threw it. The brick smashed the front windshield to pieces, with Ernest still sitting behind the wheel. He bolted from the car, threw me against the wall and hit me again and again. I clawed at his face with my hands in an attempt to protect myself. He continued hitting and punching me and left me there—a weeping, drunken, destroyed woman.

I was abominably ashamed and guilt-ridden at what had happened and was at a loss to explain my irrational behaviour. I felt as if I were fighting for my life, for my very existence. But what kind of life was this, with this man who was so cruel to me, who taught me how to be cruel? It was painfully clear that we were never meant to be together. By now I had indeed severely bonded to the trauma of our relationship. It was as if I needed trauma to survive. I could not have handled a normal, gentle life. I did not know how to fix what was happening. All I could do was cry my heart out.

He was gone five days.

We had lasted only seven months at Tregillus Street. It was time to leave.

We moved to Grovehill Road in the southwest. This time, Ernest insisted that a friend of his move in with us to save on rent. It was indeed a beautiful home, but the beauty of the home would not save us. Unbeknownst to either of us, it would be there on Grovehill Road that the relationship would finally die and the dance would finally end.

By now Joseph was just two years old and a beautiful, blond-haired, little child. His hair had lightened dramatically since birth, and it would be years before it would darken again. If there was one thing that perhaps saved my life, it was this adorable, loving, little child. I loved him more than life itself. He often came to bed with me and propped his pudgy, little legs on top of my slender back as I slept. I felt so comforted having him to love and knowing he loved me back. I did everything with him. It seemed I had finally gotten what I had always wanted—a family life. Or had I?

Ernest was back into selling dope. He was tired of always being broke and insisted on trafficking in drugs. Once again, I was devastated.

Kilos upon kilos of weed were stashed behind the ceiling panels downstairs. Low-life people trampled into my home and smoked up in the living room. They continually left through the front door, always with a kilo of weed in a brown paper bag. I became furious with the traffic and the dope-smoking in front of the baby and told Ernest it had to stop. I didn't want all those low-lifes walking in empty-handed through the front door, each leaving through the same front door, conspicuously carrying a brown paper bag. I was terrified it would be obvious to the neighbours what was going on.

So they came in through the back door. It was *810* all over again. I was powerless to stop the drug trafficking, and the fighting over the selling of drugs got worse. This was no way to raise a family and no place for a child. Ernest didn't care—he was into the money again. I was terrified I would be arrested and the baby taken from me. The lunacy had to stop.

It all ended one night after a ferocious fight. I hit Ernest, and he grabbed me and threw me to the wall. Clutching my head in his hands, he smashed my head again and again against the wall. I thought my head was going to crack and split wide open. A startling, but remarkably familiar, thought flashed through my mind:

Go ahead—kill me! I dare you to kill me!

Again and again he smashed my head hard against the wall. Blood trickled down my forehead, and Ernest, terrified, ran out the front door. It was at that moment I knew one of us was going to die, and it would probably be me. He had broken the skin of my scalp a couple of inches, and blood ran profusely. I was too ashamed to see a doctor to have the cut stitched up, so I silently washed myself up and cleaned off the wall stained with my blood.

A few days later I told my mother about the abuse. Several of my siblings came over, packed up my belongings and moved me temporarily into Mom's place. She had no idea this had been happening.

Severely traumatized, I tried to heal, to no avail.

Once again, it was time to move.

I relocated to an apartment on 16th Street and was there less than eight months. I decided to move farther west, near schools and playgrounds for Joseph. He was three and a half years old and would be starting Kindergarten in another year and a half. I was through with apartment living and knew Joey needed a nice, big yard to play in, so I moved to a duplex on 31st Street in the southwest and would not move from there for the next nine years.

Unfortunately, the fear and the terror did not leave me. I would perform a nightly ritual of barricading the doors with six or seven knives, terrified someone would break in to kill me. I would come home from work and frantically search the house in a frenzied state—

every cupboard, every closet, every corner, under every bed, in every inconceivable place that a human being could possibly hide.

Ernest was gone, but the terror had remained.

5 A Time to Weep

The grass was cool and wet, and the evening dew felt moist against my face. Shivering from the cold night air, I strained to see through the thick blackness of the night. Through the haziness, I could make out blurred, flickering stars in the sky above me. There was a slight tingling sensation in my knees. I glanced down and gasped with dismay— they were scraped and bloodied. Clumsily, I tugged at my torn stockings and ripped them off. *Oh God, how did I come to be in this wretched state?*

I was lying in a ditch—muddied, wet and freezing cold. I lay back, motionless. *What on earth had happened?* Minutes passed. A stark realization hit me and panic pulsed through my body. I trembled violently. *Oh God, where was the baby? Where did I leave the baby?*

I held my head between trembling hands. It pounded with excruciating pain. Everything was murky and terribly confusing and I couldn't think. *I prayed: God, let him be safe. Let the baby be safe. Mommy was stinking drunk again.*

I crawled through the darkness to the edge of the embankment where bright moonlight illuminated the old farmhouse in the distance, its brilliant lights casting shining, yellow rays into the yard. I strained to focus on the two dark, shadowy figures starkly lit in the open doorway.

Then I saw him.

I sighed heavily and slid back down the grassy, wet slope, my body involuntarily trembling from the cold night air. I lurched forward and violently heaved the contents of my stomach, spewing warm vomit over the grass. Again and again I heaved. I slumped to my knees, exhausted and spent, my body shaking, a searing pain ripping through my head. I had the shocking realization that this had happened before. Many times before. He would be furious with me, and there would be a terrible price to pay for what I had done.

I could hear the voices in the distance, louder now.

Unsteadily, I groped my way to the top of the embankment and stumbled to my feet as the earth spun beneath me. "There she is!" I heard someone yell. Two shapes rushed towards me, grabbed me roughly and shoved me to the ground. I struggled frantically to free myself. I felt panic, then anger. They were powerless against the incredible strength of my youthful body and unable to restrain me. I thrashed about like a trapped animal, unable to escape. More shouts. Two more officers joined in the commotion. Contorted with wild, flailing motions, I was hysterical and out of control. Hopelessly out of control. The four of them held me down.

One of the policemen yanked my arms forcefully behind my back. I heard the unmistakable clink as the handcuffs locked my wrists. As they carved into my skin, I kicked at the police officers, screaming, my body convulsing and writhing in a futile attempt to escape.

"You bastard, Ernest! You fucking bastard!" I screamed at the lone, thin figure a few yards away.

"Take her away! I want her locked up!" was the last thing I heard him say. I hated him. This ugly, little bastard who abandoned me and the baby.

The next hour was a nightmarish blur. Slumped wearily in the back seat of the patrol car, I gazed upwards as street lights swirled past the window. I was a sight for sore eyes, a fiercely intoxicated, but very attractive, twenty-one-year-old young woman.

After an eternity, the car pulled to a stop. Still appallingly drunk, I remained uncooperative as they dragged me into a building and down a long hallway, stopping along the way at an open window.

I was ordered to give up my belongings and anything I could use to hurt myself. *These freaking bastards.* A large matron led me down another hallway lined with cells and roughly uncuffed me. Finally, I was alone. Alone in a dingy, cold cement cell.

As the matron left, I screamed profanities and smashed my head again and again against the steel bars of the jail cell door. They came back, unceremoniously shoved a helmet on my head, roughly forced me into a strait-jacket and left me alone once more.

Battered and bruised, I curled up in a fetal position on the cold, damp cement floor, tears streaming down my cheeks. A burning, agonizing shame engulfed me. *Why hadn't they just let me die? That's all I really wanted. Just to be left alone to die in peace.*

I thought of my son, a beautiful, little child. He would be wondering where his Mommy was. *God, why had I done this to him again?* Exhausted and numb of any feeling, I sank into the blackness and all consciousness left me. It was a deeply troubled sleep filled with nightmarish, ghoulish sensations and tremors that racked my body throughout the night.

Hours later, morning unmercifully arrived. The relentless sounds of a screaming woman being unwillingly delivered into a nearby cell nudged me from a deeply disturbed sleep. Slowly, painfully, I opened my swollen eyes. The stark light overhead burned into me. I was still imprisoned in the strait-jacket they had forced me into just hours earlier. An overwhelming, ugly shame filled me, stinging my eyes with tears. I was horribly flawed and defective and didn't deserve to live. Perhaps the next time I would succeed in killing myself. I was alarmed and ashamed of my horribly deplorable and self-destructive thoughts, but I was unable to control them. I had felt this way for a very long time, and I could not understand or know why.

They released me a short time later with a stern admonishment. Mortified, broken and filled with shame, I stumbled down a long hallway and out into daylight. Freedom. The blinding sunlight made me cringe, and I quickened my pace, terrified of exposure. Thankfully, there was nothing to be afraid of. The streets were empty. It was just 6:30 a.m.

I rummaged in my purse for a mirror and gasped at the haggard, appalling reflection that stared back at me. I was pallid, my eyes were swollen and streaks of black mascara were smeared down my cheeks. My hair stuck to my face in damp clumps. Stripped of all dignity, I struggled to regain a sense of composure, pulled a comb through my hair and fumbled for a Kleenex to wipe the black stains from my face. I still reeked of liquor and cigarettes and a faint smell of vomit clung to my breath. I felt sick to my stomach. My head pounded with excruciating pain. It was going to be an ugly, miserable hangover.

This didn't happen. This just didn't happen, I muttered uneasily. The sun mercifully warmed my battered, shaken body as I faltered down the street. It had all been an ugly dream. I would just never think of it again. I would deny it ever happened. I was good at that. Denial.

A cab pulled up. Relieved, I got in. It was a quiet ride home as the cab driver tried unsuccessfully to engage me in conversation, occasionally glancing inquisitively at me in his rear view mirror. Certainly, I knew I was an attractive, young woman, but last night's drunken episode had taken a horrendous toll.

I had been to see Ernest earlier that evening. He had poured drinks all night, and I had proceeded to consume an incredible amount of liquor. Furious at him for abandoning me and the baby and leaving us without any financial support, I had pursued him relentlessly for months, heartbroken and unable to accept the abandonment or the lack of financial assistance. A terrible fight had broken out between us, and I had run out of the house, over the lawn and tumbled into the ditch. He had come looking for me, but I had managed to hide in the wet, muddy grass without making a sound. I just didn't care. It really didn't matter what happened to me anymore. It had been an awful mistake, seeing him last night. A mistake I had made far too many times before.

It was all too painful to think about. My head drooped in shame, and my body slumped back in the seat of the taxi. As we drew nearer to home, I brightened somewhat. It was time once again to deny another horrible night of pain. I paid the driver, silently stepped from the cab and walked slowly up the walkway to the front door.

Quietly, I turned the key in the lock and cautiously opened the door. All was silent in the semi-darkness. The heavy drapes were still drawn, and I could see young William curled up, sleeping on the couch. He was such a good babysitter. I could always trust William to take such good care of my little one.

I tip-toed softly down the hall to my son's room and silently opened his door. The tiny three-year-old lay sleeping soundly, one pudgy, little leg stretched out from beneath his blankets. I smiled weakly and listened to his peaceful breathing for a few moments. He was safe. Noiselessly, I shut his door and retreated to my bedroom across the hall. Wearily, I trembled as I undressed and stumbled into bed. A sense of security heartened me slightly as I curled up beneath the comforter. Everything was going to be okay.

The baby was safe. I was safe. No one could harm me now.

He had signed the Paternity Agreement just before Joey's third birthday.

The form had been presented to me by the Department of Maintenance and Recovery and, to my shock and amazement, had already been filled in with a grossly inadequate monthly child support of $60.00. I had had no say in the matter; $60.00 a month was not enough to feed a dog, let alone feed, clothe and maintain a growing, healthy child. Shocked at the injustice, I had argued with the Department that the woefully inadequate pittance never addressed the actual costs of maintaining my son. Bluntly, I was informed that Ernest would not pay a cent more and to either accept the $60.00 a month, or receive nothing at all.

Reluctantly, I signed the agreement without benefit of legal counsel. I could not have afforded a lawyer in any event and it was obvious that this was how the court system worked. Ernest had previously met with Maintenance and Recovery and predetermined the amount he was willing to pay, without any input by me. There was never any proper disclosure made of Ernest's financial assets, liabilities or earning capacity, nor was I ever asked to appear before a judge to speak to the actual costs of maintaining my son. The document was merely stamped by the court.

I was screwed again.

Relentlessly, I complained to the Department of Maintenance and Recovery. I felt it was grossly unfair that a substantial portion of my salary went towards supporting my son and that I was forced to pay the lion's share of the costs of raising him. After much complaining, the Department finally called to inform me they had a new agreement for me to sign. My joy abruptly turned to dismay upon realizing that the monthly support amount had been upped to a mere $100.00 a month.

Again I was shocked. Surely, I should have appeared before a judge to speak to the actual costs of supporting my son. Incredibly, Ernest had once again managed to fix the amount he was willing to pay and once again I was not asked for my input. I was furious, knowing he could well afford more than a meager $100.00 a month. It was obvious the court discriminated against unwed mothers. *Throw her a few dollars, and hopefully she'll go away.*

To make matters worse, Ernest was continually in deliberate violation of the terms of the Paternity Agreement. In 1975 there were no arrears for the three months the agreement was in effect. The following year the arrears continued for six months and Ernest gave the Department two NSF cheques.

Joseph was approximately four and a half years old when Ernest saw him for the last time. In the year previous, he had seen his son only once or twice. On that last fateful visit, Joseph was very anxious and unsure who this man called *Ernest* was. I told Ernest that his infrequent visits were doing his son more harm than good and were very traumatic on little Joey. Ernest chose not to believe me. But I was the one who had to deal with the troubled aftermath of the sporadic visits with his father and painfully witness my son revert back to infancy, babble baby talk and wet the bed night after night. It was heartbreaking to watch my little son regress to an infant state after each painful and disruptive visit with his father, a man he barely recognized. It would then be several agonizing weeks before I could pull little Joey out of his traumatized state of regression. I knew the torturous visits with Ernest had to stop, and I angrily told Ernest he was causing his son irreparable harm and to stay away if he couldn't be a full-time father to him. I made it clear Joseph needed a full-time father, not a part-time one. Ernest disagreed, but it was his ticket to freedom. He took it.

He never saw his son again.

Joseph was five years old and in Kindergarten. The painful memories of his father were beginning to fade, and Joseph appeared much happier. I knew we had both suffered severe trauma and desperately needed to heal from it. To ease my own pain, I still went out drinking and partying, and on one such occasion, I saw him for the last time.

It was Bill.

I could hardly believe my eyes. He was with Cary, and the two were in a restaurant, waiting for a table. He sauntered up to me at the bar.

"How's your son?" Bill asked. I just wanted to gush, so proud was I of little Joey.

"Oh Bill! He's just beautiful and so smart!" I wanted to take a picture out of my wallet to show him, but I didn't get the chance. Bill blurted out with a nastiness that surprised me:

"It's a miracle your son's okay with all the drugs you did." *What was this all about? What had I done to him?* I met his brashness with my own and shot back:

"So how's your brother doing?" Bill immediately shut up and glared at me. His brother, John, had overdosed on drugs two years previous and was never the same again. I knew mentioning John was insensitive, but so was what Bill had said to me. I was confounded and hurt at Bill's anger and meanness and had no idea what I had done to deserve it. Bidding me a terse good-bye, he abruptly turned his back and left. I watched him weave his way through the crowd to the other side of the restaurant to meet Cary and gazed after him until he disappeared completely from sight. In my heart, I knew I would never see Bill again. I felt an incredible sadness, and words of a beautiful, wistful song came to me.

Which way you goin' Billy?[2]
Can I go too?
Which way you goin' Billy?
Can I go with you?
I really love you Billy
And all this time
I thought you loved me Billy
And you were mine
I'm gonna miss you Billy
And though I'm tryin'
I'm hurting so bad Billy
I can't help cryin'
You are my whole babe
My heart and my soul babe
I have nothing to show babe
If you should go away
Which way you goin' Billy?
Or need I ask
'Cuz you don't want me Billy
You're free at last
I won't forget you Billy
For all my life
I'll always love you Billy
I'll stay your wife

I sat there—still, quiet, pensive. Bill was gone. Gone from my life forever. I would never forget him, nor would my thoughts ever linger far from him. It was unexplainable, but I knew it was partly because Bill was the nicest thing that happened to me before the painfully abusive relationship with Ernest destroyed my life. Bill was a lovely memory I held on to to keep me going. In time, the memory would fade to an unrealistic, silly fantasy. Just a foolish, silly fantasy of a naive, young schoolgirl.

The arrears with Ernest continued. In 1977 he was in arrears for seven months and was ordered to appear in court. The following year he was again in arrears for seven months and again had a court appearance for failure to pay child support. In 1979 he was in arrears for nine months and appeared before the court twice.

Little Joey was seven years old and in grade two. I tried to explain to him why the cheques never arrived or arrived months late, but he didn't understand. I was constantly phoning Ernest, begging him to send the money. A number of times Ernest claimed the cheque was in the mail, and foolishly believing him, I would come home night after night and frantically search the mailbox for a cheque that was never there. It was a cruel, sick joke Ernest enjoyed playing on me.

Joey needed a coat and shoes. Ernest didn't care. I couldn't afford the $40.00 to buy Joey his team soccer jacket. I was ashamed and told the coach I just didn't have the money. He was very sympathetic and understanding of my situation. Two weeks later, after getting paid for overtime, I went back to the coach and told him I could now afford the jacket. *But they were probably all gone, weren't they?* I stood there, anxiously awaiting his answer, while little Joey stood right there beside me—expectant, hopeful, waiting patiently. Smiling at us both, the coach told me to wait right there. He disappeared into his house and came back outside, proudly carrying a beautiful, brand new, cobalt-blue soccer jacket for Joey. He had saved one for me, in Joseph's size. I was so very thankful to the coach for that. Joseph was delighted. He had a team jacket like the rest of the kids.

When money did arrive, Joey and I would go on a little shopping spree to the mall to get whatever he needed. He remembered those shopping sprees for a very long time. They were important to him. He knew where the money came from.

A year passed. It was a day that I would never forget. I was in my son's bedroom, tidying up, and began looking through one of his scribblers and started reading. Suddenly, I stopped. He had been writing stories, and there, in his childlike handwriting, he had clearly printed *My father is dead.* Taken aback, I called Joey into the bedroom and showed him the scribbler. Softly, I spoke to him.

"Joey, why have you written your father is dead?" His answer stunned me.

"Mom, it's a lot easier to tell people he's dead than to try to explain where he is."

Oh God. I was shocked. *This out of a precious, little eight-year-old child.* "Joey, you know your father isn't dead. He lives in Lethbridge."

"Then why doesn't he see me, Mom?" he asked in a sad, plaintive, little voice. I tried to explain that Ernest had a new family in Lethbridge and that I didn't know why he didn't see him. Then it hit me, hard.

"You mean you've told people that he's dead?" I stared at him incredulously. The worried expression on his little face spoke volumes. "The teachers too?" I asked him. My mouth dropped open in shock. *I had always wondered why no one had ever asked me about my husband or Joey's father. Not once. Not ever. Now I knew.*

My precious, little child. He was terrified, and his little voice quivered as he begged me:

"Mom, please don't make me go back and tell them he isn't dead." There was an incredible look of anguish on his face, and my heart ached for my little son who stood there so gallantly in front of me. All I had to do was look at him, and I melted with the love I felt so deeply for him. My voice was soothing as I comforted him.

"No, my little sweetheart. You don't have to go back and tell them anything different at all. But no more writing in your scribblers that your father is dead. Okay? Can you promise me that?" There was a look of immense relief on his face as he agreed. I grabbed him and held him tight to me. *I don't know why he doesn't see you Joey. I just don't know.* I couldn't let go of him, and he clung to me.

My heart broke at that moment and holding my precious, little child tightly, I vowed to do everything in my power to make him forget all about Ernest and the pain and the trauma. I would do everything in my power to give my son the happiest childhood ever. I did not know at the time that I had managed to bandage up his pain—the pain of abandonment by his father. Pain he so desperately needed to feel. I took that pain from him. It was what was needed for us to survive.

We never spoke of Ernest again.

The arrears continued.

In 1980 Ernest was in arrears for the better part of the year and appeared in court for failure to pay child support. The same thing happened in 1981 and 1982. Finally, he was in arrears for the first five consecutive months of 1983.

I couldn't take it anymore.

Joey was ten years old when I canceled the Paternity Agreement. I called the Department of Maintenance and Recovery and told them it just wasn't working and to cancel the agreement. It gave us more trauma than anything else—waiting for cheques that were several months late or never arrived at all. The social worker told me that it was Joseph's money, not mine, and that he had a right to it. Very matter-of-factly I informed the worker, "It's no one's money if no one gets it." Reluctantly, he agreed with me. Ernest had shirked his moral and legal responsibility to jointly support his child. The Paternity Agreement had always been unjust and unreasonable, and I had always paid the lion's share of raising Joseph. A mere pittance of $100.00 a month, if we ever received it, wasn't worth the trauma it brought both Joseph and I. The social worker understood. We had been through too much.

The connection was broken. The tie was severed.

Joseph was worried when I told him that night. "Mom, are we going to be broke?" he asked in a worried, sweet, little voice. My heart melted.

"No, sweetie-pie. I'll work extra overtime, and I'll make up the money. We're not going to be broke. Not at all." He seemed a little relieved, but I could tell he was sad. It was the final connection to his father, a man he hadn't seen in over five years. The tie to his father had finally been severed. He was grieving for him. He was grieving for his lost father.

I let him grieve.

It would be years before we healed from the trauma we had endured.

6 *The Game*

Young Joseph and I struggled on alone.

Frequently I brought my son over to Mom's for the weekend, thinking that if she couldn't love me, perhaps she could love my son. Somehow, I felt as if I were sending him in my place because I had never found my place in that family. Perhaps he could. Mom would often comment that she felt like Joey was 'her child' or 'one of her own', a remark that always left me feeling very uncomfortable and confused.

My youngest sister Josephine still lived at home and continually overstepped the limits I tried to set with her when I left my son with Mom. She would argue and become angry with me when I made plans with Joey, insisting she had already made arrangements with my son to spend time with her. She would not consult me, nor would she ask my consent before doing so. I began to tire of her contempt and disrespect towards me and decided I had had enough the day she argued with me over taking my son on a trip. The controversy lasted a week, and I made the mistake of giving in to her.

Admittedly, at the time I did not fully understand the psychology of healthy boundaries or equally unhealthy enmeshment, but I instinctively knew my sister's relationship with my son was not healthy. It had instead become an unhealthy entanglement, and I related my concern to Mom. To my shock and dismay, she angrily demanded to know if I was accusing my sister of sexually abusing my son. *Good Grief. Didn't either of them recognize that my son and I were a family, separate and apart from them? Couldn't they see that, as a family, my son and I needed time together?*

Although I was acutely aware of my need to be independent and to have a life of my own, knowing intuitively it was perfectly normal and healthy, I felt I was not allowed to leave my family of origin to raise a family of my own. Did my mother and sister honestly think I would go and live my life and leave my son behind with them?

Deeply troubled and disheartened by the inexplicable feeling of enmeshment I felt with various family members, I began to see that the bonding between family members was not a healthy one, nor were there any healthy boundaries to speak of. Everyone minded in everyone else's business. It was as if we were one large, undifferentiated mass of people, incapable of independent thought or action, and any attempt to attain autonomy by leaving the family was met with a strong and angry resistance.

The pull of the family was inexorably strong, and it was as if I were constantly being sucked into a vortex that I fought valiantly to free myself from. Although it was a tremendous struggle, I pulled away with my son to be free and to have a life separate and apart from the rest of them. Josephine never forgave me for that. Frankly, I didn't give a damn. I knew my son and I needed to be a healthy family unit far more than my son needed to be enmeshed with his unhealthy aunt.

Years later, after Josephine had married, she invited me more than once for Christmas dinner at her home. When I would calmly inform her I had other plans, she would demand of me irately, "Then let Joey come!" *So my young son was supposed to spend Christmas with his aunt instead of his own mother?* I realized it wasn't me she wanted for dinner, but rather it was my son. I was just an irritating and unwelcome attachment to him. Her contempt and hostility towards me took me by surprise and would, in time, cause a permanent rift between us.

I immersed myself in work, putting in hundreds of hours of overtime, to ensure there would be enough money to pay for rent, food and bills. I had promised my son that we would never be broke, and I could not break that promise to him. Nothing was more important to me than making sure he had the happiest childhood possible, something I could not ever remember having myself. I did not mind working the overtime hours. It enabled me to afford to pay for his soccer, Little League and Big League baseball, hockey, skiing and figure skating. He was outfitted with equipment for all the summer sports as well as for various winter sports. I participated alongside him and skied and skated with him. Spending the day with him on the mountains was invigorating, and it became evident to me that my son was a natural-born athlete on the slopes. Nothing gave me more pleasure than spending my time with him and watching him thrive.

I enrolled Joseph in a modeling course to increase his self-esteem, and although there were only a couple of events he participated in, it was exciting and challenging for him. There was also kayaking and canoeing as well as a YMCA Day Camp. We both loved the YMCA Day Camp because it was located downtown, and I could pick him up right after work. That became the most enjoyable part of my day, and he would be so happy to see me. He spent time away from me at a summer camp, and it was very difficult on both of us for him to be away for extended periods of time. I encouraged Joseph to join the local scout troop, believing it would help in developing his interpersonal skills with other young lads, and outfitted him with scouting equipment.

Having swam as a youngster myself, I enrolled Joseph in competitive swimming with the Killarney Swim Club. He swam with the club for seven years, and I continued to work hard to pay for yearly dues, boot camps, swimsuits, trips, entry fees, competition fees and a plane trip to Vancouver for a provincial swim meet. I could not have been prouder of Joseph's accomplishments. He acquired his Senior Resuscitation, Bronze Medallion, Bronze Cross, Award of Distinction, Award of Merit, Life Saving I, II and III, and finally, he achieved his National Lifeguard status. I was always at the pool and proudly watched him swim his first mile, all the while cheering him on. I baked treats for swim meets and timed swimmers at the end of the pool alongside other parents.

I went to every soccer and hockey game, and we flooded the backyard one winter so Joseph could skate every night. He became an accomplished skater, and the figure skating helped his hockey game. He outshone the others in baseball and proved to be a natural. I often told my son he did not have to be better than anyone else, but rather he should be the best he could be. As I watched my energetic, little son grow and excel in every sport, he surpassed my every expectation and I was filled with an immense feeling of satisfaction and fulfillment. I was as proud as any mother could have been.

I had succeeded. He had forgotten. He had forgotten all about the trauma. Little did I realize we would have to revisit it again some-day.

He would crawl into bed every night, exhausted. I would snuggle next to him, and we would discuss the day's events. Those moments were precious to both of us. As the wind blew gently through his open window, we would lay there and chatter away, warm and snug beneath his comforter. It didn't matter what we discussed; what mattered was that we were together. I knew he loved me deeply and would impishly whine when I got up to leave. No matter how tired or weary I was from a long day at work, I never begrudged my nightly presence with my son, knowing full well that if I did not spend those precious moments with him, they could never be relived and would be lost forever. So I savoured them, knowing he would always remember.

He had difficulty reading and writing in the early years at school, and I spent hundreds of hours working with him, having him write and re-write words he misspelled. Repeating words over and over forced him to work harder at the language to fully grasp it. I had not heard of dyslexia, but if he indeed suffered from it, I would learn many years later that I had handled the situation correctly. If I had neglected to spend the time studying with him, his reading and writing abilities would have remained at a junior high level. There came a time when I accidentally misspelled a word, and he caught my mistake, and it was his turn to make me write the word out twenty times. We both laughed at that because I rarely made a spelling mistake. It was perhaps one of the few things I had actually enjoyed and excelled at in school—reading and English. So I read to Joey, and when he was older, he read to me. We read *Winnie the Pooh* together, and both of us cried when I turned the last page and the book was finished. After that, I called him my 'little pookin', coined after the little bear in the book.

Not only was it my responsibility to ensure my son's emotional development, but also his intellectual development, and so I made sure I was present at every parent-teacher interview through grade 12. Joseph had begun to excel in school, particularly in Mathematics. His math teacher informed me that Joseph was very talented in Math and urged me to encourage him to continue on with it in university. There was a problem, however, and he asked me if I was going through a divorce or a major upheaval in my life or was I having some other difficulty at home.

Young Joseph was misbehaving badly in school. I was shocked as one teacher after another spoke to me about his appalling behaviour. The women teachers loved him and attested to his genuinely well-behaved conduct, obedience and helpfulness in class. They confirmed he was a joy to have around and that he often volunteered to stay late after class to clean the chalkboards. His male teachers, however, told an entirely different story. I was astounded and dismayed to hear that Joseph repeatedly and boldly defied them, argued that they had incorrectly arrived at a specific solution and generally behaved as if he were superior to them in his knowledge of a particular subject. On numerous occasions he had been kicked out of class and made to sit in the hall for his impudence and hostility towards more than one of his male teachers. He challenged and generally antagonized the hell out of them. I told Joseph's teachers I would handle the situation and that if he gave them any more trouble, to tell him they would be contacting his mother.

I was furious by the time I got home from the parent-teacher interviews and confronted my son with his atrocious behaviour. It was obvious by the gender differentiation that young Joseph was having great difficulty accepting male authority. I lectured him for well over an hour about treating all of his teachers with respect, regardless of their gender. They were not there to be disrespected or questioned with regards to their teaching methods—certainly not by a pupil. I believe I got my point across, for I never heard another complaint from any of Joseph's male teachers again. All they had to do was mention my name and young Joseph smartened up at once.

There was, however, something very different about Joseph that had been worrying me for some time. I had noticed early on that he appeared to lag behind his friends' emotional level of intelligence, and so I did my best to teach him. I felt as if I were dragging him behind me, and I was afraid that if I let go of him, he would be stuck and unable to move. There were times I just wanted to grab hold and shake him to get a reaction out of him. A part of him was severely repressed, and I could not pry it loose. It was as if he were insulated against his emotions and feelings, and so I did everything I could to make him feel good about himself. But there was something deeper lurking inside him that I was unable to touch. He tried to hide it from me, but I always knew it was there.

Joseph graduated grade 12 with honours and achieved the Baccalaureate Program in Math. I could not have been prouder of my young son.

The emotional problems with Joseph got worse, and we fought constantly. On one such occasion, he screamed at me in rage:

"I have so much anger in me—you must have abused me!" I was stunned and shaken by his accusation. *Abused him? I loved him more than life itself.*

I had always intuitively known that something about my son was amiss, but I could never fully discern what it was or how I could fix it. I began to wonder if my son's anger had something to do with being abandoned by his father, and consequently I mentioned Ernest to him. Joseph was furious at the mere mention of his name. I knew the time was not yet right to deal with it, and so I left it alone.

I endured endless confrontations with my son and began to feel sorry for him, knowing that emotionally, something about him was not right. I was burdened with enormous guilt that he hadn't had a father, and Joseph learned very quickly to play on that guilt and continually used it against me in an attempt to manipulate me into getting what he wanted. If I didn't comply with his wishes, he withdrew his love and treated me with contempt and scorn.

Worst of all, he betrayed me with family members, one by one.

On several occasions I gave my older brother Joe money to enable my son to go to Idaho on a vacation with him, his wife and their two boys. Although I could not really afford the vacations for myself, I wanted my son to go and have a good time. Inevitably, when he returned home, I would be treated with terrible disrespect and scorn. He once jeered at me:

"You can't afford a boat. You can't even afford a decent vacation for me."

I was hurt and shocked by his insolence and began to wonder if my son thought I wasn't good enough for him or if what I was able to provide good enough either. I regretted giving my permission for the trips to Idaho, and finally one year, I had had enough and refused to let him go. I no longer wanted him to accompany his uncle and cousins on any more vacations and attempted to explain my reasons to my sister Patricia.

"You're selfish! If you don't let him go, you're just being selfish!

Her words stung sharply, and against my better judgment, I gave in. It would be the last summer vacation my son would spend with his relatives, but this time, things would be very different. I would join the group on this final excursion, and I would find out once and for all exactly what went on during those yearly trips to Idaho that transformed my son into a miserable, uncontrollable brat.

What I experienced on that doomed vacation would affect me for years to come.

We arrived in Idaho after traveling a long and exhausting day. My son, at the outset of the vacation, disappeared after I had given him express instructions to help me buy groceries for the next two weeks. Concerned, I told my brother Joe I couldn't find my son. To my surprise, he shrugged me off and answered loftily:

"I told them they could go and play videos." I was annoyed at my brother and replied matter-of-factly:

"Well, I didn't."

My son miraculously reappeared after I had finished shopping. I was angry and accosted him with the lack of responsibility he had displayed in defying my instructions. I would not have tolerated such behaviour at home, and I would certainly not tolerate it here in Idaho. My son retaliated with words that cut into me like a razor-sharp knife.

"As far as I am concerned, Uncle Joe is my guardian out here—not you."

I winced in pain at his words, completely taken aback by his shameful and vicious outburst. I felt sick to my stomach. *Not only did my brother not recognize or respect me as my son's mother, but also my own son.* Finally, I understood what happened on those vacations.

From that moment on, everything went pretty much downhill. My brother did not allow me to have a say in anything that happened during the entire two-week vacation. I was not even permitted to use the campsite I paid for. Instead, and without any explanation, Joe insisted that I set up my tent directly behind his motor home. I was frustrated and angry and could not understand why he would not allow me to stake my tent on the site I had paid for. Upon questioning, he became extremely annoyed with me and brusquely told me that he was saving my site for other cousins he had invited. The campground had run out of camping lots, and he had given them mine. I was angry and hurt, not because Joe had given my campsite away to cousins that would be arriving the following day, but because he had not asked my permission to do so. It was obvious he was the boss out here, and he made that abundantly clear to me the following morning when he sternly lectured me as if I were a child.

"You're not going to ruin my vacation." Funny, I thought it was my vacation as well.

My nephews were impudent and cocky and controlled the entire vacation from beginning to end. My brother and his wife did all the cooking, laundry and cleaning up after their sons, who lifted not one finger to help. I could not possibly have allowed my son to behave in the same manner as his cousins and insisted he wash the dishes and clean up with me after each meal. I would have expected no less of him at home and saw no reason for it to be different out here. But it was a tiresome and grueling battle. My son was frequently obnoxious and felt he should be entitled to the same special treatment his cousins received.

To make matters worse, Joe and his wife Evelyn ridiculed me for directing my son to clean up. Instead, they allowed their boys to run off after every meal to play. The two brothers amused themselves with a video game called *Nintendo* in their parents' plush motor home for hours or, when they tired of that, demanded money and were given either a ten- or twenty-dollar bill to spend on the video terminals in the camp's recreational building. In contrast, I could only afford to give my son a quarter or two. I did not have that kind of money to lavishly throw away, and it horrified me that my brother's children wasted so much hard-earned cash on video games. The boys would disappear in the boat for hours without any consideration given whatsoever to waiting for me or their parents to join them, even though I had expressly given my brother money for gas for the boat. It was a hell of a struggle attempting to keep my son in line, and in no time at all, I tired of the whole lot of them.

I had watched my nephews sulk to get their way, and I had witnessed their parents' continual indulgence of their demands. Weary of it all, I looked forward to the end of the vacation and going home.

Finally, it was the day before we were to leave.

My brother and his wife were out on the boat, and I was the only adult left behind with my son and the other kids on the beach. My youngest nephew Cory started a fight with my son. He was trying to break Joseph's sunglasses, so Joseph twisted Cory's arm to prevent him from doing so. Initially, I pleaded with Cory to let go of the glasses. Having just paid $85.00 for the designer sunglasses as a present for my son, I could ill-afford to buy another pair. Cory ignored my pleadings, and in a raised voice, I finally ordered him to let go of the glasses. Whimpering, he did.

His fifteen-year-old brother Little Joe was furious that I had dared tell Cory what to do, and he raised his voice and shouted at me:

"Cory could pay for those sunglasses if he broke them because Cory has lots of money!" Flustered with Little Joe's impudence, I informed him that it was not okay for Cory to break something that wasn't his. Little Joe became even more belligerent and bellowed at me:

"It's okay if Cory breaks the glasses because we have lots of money and we can easily buy another pair!"

That did it. I had had enough of those two brats, particularly Little Joe. I had patiently shut up for the past two weeks, and I could not be silent any longer.

"Why don't you zip your lip!" I shot angrily at my nephew. Little Joe was furious with me and retaliated in a sarcastic voice:

"Why don't you zip yours?" I was infuriated that Little Joe dared to speak back to me so contemptuously and I yelled at him:

"You may speak to your parents like that, but don't you dare talk to me like that! You're a spoilt brat!" Defiant, Little Joe tried to yell back at me, but I interrupted him in a powerful, commanding voice.

"Stop it, Little Joe! Stop it right now!" Fuming, he finally shut up, furiously got up, grabbed his younger brother Cory and stormed off. *Good riddance. The miserable, little brats were gone.*

A short time later my brother and his wife returned from their boat ride and I calmly told them what had transpired. I honestly thought my brother would chastise his son for his rude behaviour. To my shock, my brother immediately walked over to his son's fifteen-year-old friend and questioned him in a subdued voice, thinking I wouldn't hear.

"So what really happened here?"

I was dumbfounded. *What was going on? I was his sister. Wasn't my story good enough for him? Why did he have to consult a fifteen-year-old kid?* My sister-in-law Evelyn, emotionally wrought and in tears, hurried off to find her two boys.

I felt extremely uncomfortable and told my brother I was going back to the campsite and instructed my son to pack up and accompany me.

Unexpectedly, I ran into my incredibly agitated sister-in-law and nephews. Evelyn proceeded to yell at me.

"I left Little Joe in charge of Cory, not you!" *What? Was Little Joe, an insolent fifteen-year-old kid, in charge of me, an adult, as well?*

Reeling at her outrageous outburst, I calmly replied, "He lipped me off, Evelyn." Her son, Little Joe, at her side, yelled venomously, "I did not!"

Evelyn continued shouting harshly, "You must have done something to my son to have made him do any such thing!"

I stood there in disbelief. Calmly, I said, "We'll just leave, Evelyn." To my dismay, she screamed maliciously:

"Good! Go! Get out of here! You're driving us all crazy—especially the way you treat your son!"

Caught off-guard by her explosive attack, I was too stunned to reply. Her son, Little Joe, savagely ripped his father's camera from my hand, shouting, "Give me back my camera!" I was astonished that his irascible behaviour went unchecked yet again by his mother. The little brat screamed one final insult:

"I want my car back!"

I felt nauseated that Little Joe would demand back an old beat-up car his father had given me, having mistakenly believed the debt to my brother had been repaid. Realizing the utter hopelessness of the situation, I silently turned to go. I was totally shattered by what had just happened and walked, shaken, back to the car with my son. Together we drove back to the campsite.

Horribly distraught, I instructed Joseph to help me pack up our tent and belongings. I was a nervous wreck and just wanted to get the hell out of there. My son became visibly angry and wanted to stay. *After all that just happened?* He didn't care. Apparently, he had made arrangements to meet a young girl that evening down by the beach, and I had spoilt things for him. To punish me, he treated me miserably and was sullen all the way home.

Forced to travel through the mountains in pitch blackness, I gripped the steering wheel until my knuckles turned white and prayed that none of the huge logging trucks would squash us under their gigantic wheels as they thundered around the tight mountain curves. It was an unbearably exhausting eight-hour drive home, and I was thankful to make it back alive. The old car blew its transmission shortly after the long journey, and I felt like depositing the piece of junk on my brother's lawn for his spoilt, ungrateful son. But Little Joe was far too good to be seen in an old wreck that I had been only too thankful to drive.

There would be no more vacations with my brother or his children. Everything had become painfully clear to me, and I realized with unmistakable clarity why my son returned from those vacations an uncontrollable, spoilt brat. I should never have permitted him to join my brother and his family for vacations all those years. It had been a big mistake and one I would regret for the rest of my life.

Later the following day, I received the startling news. My brother had returned home and maliciously bad-mouthed me to the rest of the family, telling them I was crazy and should be locked up. I felt I needed to defend myself and, with the assistance of my older brother Brian, drafted a defense letter which I sent to various members of the family, relating my side of the story.

The letter infuriated my brother Joe. I had exposed him and his family, and I had dared speak the truth about his sons' appalling behaviour. For that, I would have to be severely punished, and my brother would find a way to do just that.

I spoke to my son about what had happened, and he confided to me that his cousin Little Joe bragged to him that if he ever wanted to get anything from his father, all he had to do was sulk in his room, and my brother Joe, to persuade his son to come out, would promise to buy him whatever he wanted. If Little Joe wanted something more elaborate or expensive, he only had to sulk a little longer. It was no way to raise a child, and I knew it was wrong. I made it clear to my son that the way I was treated by my brother, his wife and their two boys on that ghastly vacation was not right and that I would not tolerate being treated like that again, by any member of my family.

I insisted on loyalty from my son, but he steadfastly refused to give it to me. How could my son and I be a family without loyalty? He continued to betray me with almost every member of my family and refused to admit his cousin had been insolent to me that day on the beach and even went so far as denying he remembered anything at all about the day's shocking events.

The betrayal happened again. With a sister. Then again with another sister-in-law. Apparently, certain people in my family decided I was indeed crazy and they encouraged my son to get away from me and invited him to come and live with them. I do not know if my son manipulated members of my family into believing I was crazy or if my brother did so out of the contemptible abhorrence he felt towards me. I only knew it was profoundly objectionable and disgraceful for family members to treat me as they did. And I knew it had to stop.

As time went on, Joseph gained the upper hand and managed to assert enormous power and control over me, while I grappled with regaining my self-esteem after every exhausting fight with him. I weakened with the continual fighting, and he grew stronger, exhorting in his triumphant game of manipulation, exploitation and guilt. I finally recognized that it was indeed a game he was playing with me. I was a player in that game, struggling to remain on the game board without being knocked off. Either I battled to get back onto the game board and fought valiantly to stay in the game, or my son lured me back into the game with his charm and manipulations. Either way, I was hopelessly locked in a dangerous game of deceit and lies that would not end.

For the next several years, Joseph continued the manipulation game with me, and the fighting increased. It became very damaging to my spirit as I fought and struggled to have control and power over my own life, and he sought to destroy that. He wanted me to take care of him, and I desperately needed my independence from him. He would shout in rage at me:

"It's your duty! You're my mother! You brought me into this world—you owe me!" I was dazed by his outbursts and could not understand where he got such a powerfully and incredibly inaccurate notion of entitlement. I did recognize that his scornfulness and disrespect towards me was emotionally and psychologically abusive. Unfortunately, I had not yet fully comprehended and come to terms with the fact that I still carried abandonment fears from childhood that forced me back into the game again and again, allowing the abusive power play to continue. Nor did I understand at the time that Joseph's participation in the game was in response to his anger at being abandoned by a father—something that was beyond his control. The game, however, was something he could control. And control it he did. I was powerless to stop the game, and in many respects, it felt remarkably similar to the dance, all over again.

The betrayals worsened. My son lied to me one evening about where he was going and my sister Joan secretly invited him to my brother Joe's for dinner. I found out and was furious with her. An awful fight ensued over the phone, and Joan, stinking drunk, yelled to my mother that I was indeed crazy and that my son should come and live with her in Toronto *(on welfare, no less)*. It would be years before Joan and I spoke again and, even then, only once or twice. The close relationship we had once shared had been irreparably damaged.

My brother Joe continued to invite my son for dinners behind my back, and my son continued to lie to me about going to them. He would sneer at me whenever I told him how much it hurt me. Joseph's deceitful behaviour caused terrible fights between us, and I began to recognize that that was my brother's intention all along. For the life of me, I couldn't understand how my brother Joe could be so sadistic and deliberately hurt me with such shameful cruelty. No one could possibly convince me he was doing it out of love for me.

There was a huge family reunion, and everyone who was even remotely related to our family was invited, including my son. I was the only one excluded from the big reunion organized by my brother and held at his home. Unexpectedly, I found out that my son had lied to me and secretly attended the reunion behind my back. He did not care that his own mother was the only one specifically and maliciously excluded from it. My mother went as far as instructing my mentally handicapped brother Michael to lie to me about my son being at the gathering and further instructed a remote cousin to also lie to me about meeting my son at the reunion. Everything was kept a big secret from me. My brother and the others surreptitiously and successfully enjoined my son to take part in the secret and the lie with them. I was crushed by my son's and family's betrayal and lies and realized that these were sick people, intent on keeping me in my rigid, dysfunctional role as the Family Scapegoat.

My brother had indeed found a cruel, sick way to punish me. And punish me he did, again and again. Joe's dinners continued in secret behind my back, and my son shamelessly attended each one of them and lied to me afterwards.

If I was devastated by my brother's ruthlessness towards me, I was even more horrified by my son's betrayal, lies and disloyalty. Angry at everything my brother had done to hurt me, I finally decided to confront him and telephoned him one afternoon in an attempt to force everything out into the open.

Little Joe, the nephew I had fought with that fateful day on the beach in Idaho, answered the phone. He was rude to me, refused to let me speak, laughed loudly with contempt into the phone and abruptly hung up on me. Undeterred, I phoned back, and this time his mother answered and shockingly repeated her son's boorish behaviour. I was appalled. *This was a loving, caring family?*

Distraught, I walked by the river for hours and attempted to make sense of the mess. If I did not find some kind of solace, I knew my brother would succeed in destroying me.

I decided to try to speak to Joe once more and telephoned him for the last time. Thankfully, he answered the phone. Shaking with anger, I confronted him.

"Joe, what you did to me was hurtful. You had no right to purposely invite my son behind my back."

He answered sardonically and in a patronizing voice as if he were scolding a child, "Oh now, Maureen, we don't want any trouble here." Furious, I yelled at him:

"Fuck off, Joe!" and slammed down the phone. I was at a public phone at the boat yard, and people stopped dead in their tracks to stare at me in disbelief. It didn't matter. I said what I had so desperately needed to say and walked away.

It was over.

My brother and I would never speak again.

7 *The Secret*

I had taken up watercolour painting while Joseph was still a child and it had, through the years, brought a measure of solace and comfort to my otherwise tumultuous life. It was probably the only thing that kept me sane. I craved serenity in my life, and painting gave that to me. It provided me with the motivation to put an end to the hectic and chaotic lifestyle I had previously maintained—a lifestyle that was no longer tenable and which I could no longer sustain.

It all began on a cold, snowy Saturday afternoon in February of 1994. I had gotten the paints out and set about putting pigment to paper. Vibrant colours merged and mingled on the textured fibers, and with an experienced hand, I glazed various areas, allowing underlying layers to shine through. The design of the work gradually took hold, and two hours later, the painting finished, I stopped to inspect it. It was indeed a lovely work of art.

So what! Who cares—it's just a painting.

What was I saying? What was wrong with me? Why was I so indifferent and so totally detached to the work I had just created? The thought was out of my head before I could stop it.

God, please reveal to me the reason for my feeling of incompleteness.

A week later it was artists' night with the society I belonged to, and I looked forward to getting out for the meeting. I sat next to a stranger that night. Alice noticed my last name written in my binder and looked at me inquisitively.

"Do you have a brother named Brendan?" Her question took me by surprise.

"Yes, I do. He's my eldest brother."

"I'm Alice. I used to date your brother back in Toronto in 1967." *Good God. Perhaps she could shed some light on what had happened to him. He had always lived such a sorry, sad existence.*

"What was he like back then?" I asked curiously. She answered me, very matter-of-factly:

"Well, he was depressed and very angry. He felt betrayed—you know—because of your mother's religion and all."

Betrayed? Religion? She was giving me a very important clue and I didn't get it.

I stared at her blankly. She explained:

"You know. Because your mother was pregnant before she got married to your father. Brendan felt very betrayed by that—you know—on account of your mother's religion and all."

What? Pregnant before she got married? My mother? I tried to hide my astonishment at her words.

"Oh, right. Of course." Inside, I was screaming.

The ugly shame! That's where I got it from—my mother. I carried that loathsome shame all my life, and it was never my burden to carry. I have to get out of here.

I was going to be sick. I managed to speak to Alice for a few minutes longer and told her my brother was not a very healthy man, nor had he been for most of his sorry, sad life.

My world had just shattered. My head was reeling. I was confused, angry, sad and in shock.

And mother had called me a slut when I was still a virgin. There was also the time she finally visited my father's grave with me when I told her of my nightmares. It was there, sitting on my father's grave, that she had told me that sex before marriage was like 'dogs doing it.' I remember how her words had stung sharply and I had felt that familiar revulsion—that ugly, loathsome shame. *I had had sex and never been married. What did that make me?* Always, always, it was the same ugly, loathsome, vile shame. Her shame—not mine. She had given it to me, and I had not only been burdened with it, but I had also acted it out destructively for years.

I got home, still in shock, and knew I needed to call Mom and ask her if it was true. It just didn't make sense. She had always told us sex before marriage was an ugly, dirty sin. How could she have been so hypocritical? And how had that affected poor Brendan, being the first born? I had always felt he was filled with shame and he had, on more than one occasion, said pitifully to Mom:

"I'll make you proud of me yet, mother." *He was a fifty-year-old man still yearning for his mother's approval. Why, in God's name?*

I was extremely nervous when I picked up the phone. "Mom, I met someone tonight. Someone from the past. Is it true you were pregnant before you got married?"

Dead silence. There was not a sound. Oh God, it was true!

"Mom?" I asked anxiously.

"Who told you that?" she demanded angrily.

"Just an artist friend. Someone who used to date Brendan a long time ago." I paused. "Is it true?" To my horror, she raged at me:

"My parents told me if I married your father I was as good as dead, and they'd even put the nails in the coffin!"

Oh God, what have I done? There was fury in her voice as she continued to lash out at me.

"Do you know they didn't even help me pay for his funeral? Did you know the neighbours collected money to help me bury him? Did you know that? My own parents didn't help me!"

What on earth did any of this have to do with what I had asked her? I was stunned. *What the hell was going on?* Nervous, I accidentally giggled.

"Why are you laughing at me?" she demanded to know in a crazed voice.

Immediately, I regressed back in time and was once again a small, terrified child. The angry voice I was hearing was unmistakably that of the raging, violent mother I remembered so well as a child—the voice of the woman I had been so terrified of. Frantically, I tried to explain myself.

"Mom, I'm not laughing at you. It's just that I realize you're as human as the rest of us. That's all." She was still enraged.

"Why did you ask me that? Why did you have to ask me that?" *It was a secret she had intended to take to the grave with her, and I had unexpectedly unearthed that secret.*

Feebly, I attempted to explain myself and hurriedly got off the phone. I felt destroyed by the horrible, venomous rage she had just vented at me. Reeling, I staggered the few steps to a living room chair and sank weakly into it. My heart and soul ached with unspeakable grief, and my body convulsed with unendurable pain.

This is what had happened to me. This is how it all began. I cried for the little girl I once was, the little girl who had been so destroyed by this raging, angry, violent, emotionally crippled woman. My soul wept in agony. I mourned the death of that sweet, innocent, little child I once was.

My grief continued for months on end. There was much to grieve for.

It would be two years before I could forgive mother for what she had done. I had spent years in destructive relationships with men— some abusive, some violent, all severely emotionally detached. Now, I not only understood the self-destructive behaviour patterns that pervaded my life like a poison, but also the origin. I had finally been blessed with awareness, and recovery could finally begin.

Fervently, I began studying psychology and got into therapy for treatment of family of origin issues. The discovery of my mother's secret shattered what is known in psychology as the 'fantasy bond'—a seemingly indestructible bond that binds us to unhealthy parents through the idealization of them as loving, caring people. I could now recognize my mother as the emotionally damaged woman she truly was and I could now, finally, stop futilely searching for the love she would never be able to give.

It was time for me to love and heal myself.

On my son's birthday, I wrote a letter to mother.

Dear Mom:

I am writing this letter because I need to let you know how I feel.

I understand now how hard it has been for you to express your true emotions to me. I mistakenly thought we could talk about anything when I asked you about your secret and I now realize how wrong I was. In functional families, things are talked about openly, not suppressed or denied. In our family, that has never been the case. I believe you felt your emotions through me, which has not been healthy for me. I needed to know how you felt, but you have never been able to express yourself to me. I really don't know anything about you—your past or your family. I think this is very sad, but I know there is nothing I can do about that.

I will not allow you to put your shame, your blame or your guilt on me again. Nor will I allow anyone else in the family, particularly Brian, to do so either. I will not be the Scapegoat for this family any longer.

You did your best. I am acutely aware of that. I have always appreciated everything you have ever done for me.

I love you, but I also love myself, and I now need to focus my energy on my life and that of my son. I owe us that.

I will always love you mother, but I realize we both need time to ourselves. I sincerely hope that sometime in the future we can talk about things openly and honestly, without blame, shame or guilt.

Maureen

Mother wrote back:

Thank you for your letter. It must have taken some time and soul-searching to write, and I appreciate you letting me know how you feel. I think you did an excellent job raising Joey on your own. I do not feel, however, that you were used as a scapegoat. I've always been supportive and been there for you.

Yes, I know I've made mistakes—we all have. In making decisions as a parent, one usually converses with his or her spouse. Being a single parent myself, with no family here, I had no one to voice my concerns or problems. Therefore, I suppressed talking openly. As far as my childhood goes, I have no fond memories. Now, after thirty-four years, you want me to talk openly and express how I feel.

I know it has been difficult for you, as it has been for all of us, and I think your decision to take time for yourself and Joey is a good one.

Maureen, I love you and I always have. In the future, however, and if this offends you I'm sorry, I do not wish to discuss the past as it causes too much pain.

Mother

I read and re-read her letter. It did nothing but disturb me. What was all this about thirty-four years? What was that all about? What happened thirty-four years ago? I sat there, deep in thought, counting back the years.

Suddenly, it struck me, hard.

No, it couldn't be! That was the year her husband died—thirty-four years ago in 1960. She was still back there. She had not moved a day since.

Her letter spoke volumes. Mother had been emotionally repressed for the last thirty-four years of her life. I had inadvertently touched her pain, and she had reacted violently with me. And now she was warning me to leave it alone. So be it. She could have her pain. She could wallow in it for the rest of her days, and that would be fine with me. I had more important things to do with my life than to be sucked into the vortex of her suffering. I had tried so very, very hard to love her, but she refused to let me get close to her. She may as well have jumped into the grave after her husband that sorrowful day in June so many years ago. *What the heck—that was the day she had died anyway.*

I wept relentlessly and mourned my mother's death. Yet she was very much alive.

8 *The End of the Beginning*

Several months had passed since the altercation with my mother. It was May of 1994. Joseph was twenty-one years old, still in university and had been living on his own for over a year.

The day began like any other. I was at work, perusing through family law cases that regularly came across my desk. Suddenly, something jumped out at me from the case I was reading. A woman had been awarded arrears for child maintenance dating back ten years pursuant to the *Maintenance and Enforcement Act*. No such Act had been in existence at the time I fought so laboriously for support. Although I had heard about the new Act two years previous, I was unaware it was retroactive ten years prior to its enactment.

It was time to go back to the beginning to end it.

I phoned the old, familiar Department of Maintenance and Recovery and anxiously told a family maintenance worker who I was and asked if they still had my old file. She would check and get back to me. Later that day the worker telephoned to tell me she had found the old file in storage, dusted it off, photocopied the relevant documentation needed to file an application and put everything in the mail for me.

A few days later the package arrived. Nervously, I perused through old records enumerating years of delinquent payments and court attendances for failure to pay child support. There were old copies of Ernest's letters in his familiar handwriting written to the

Department claiming he was nearly penniless and unable to pay child support. A terrible feeling of injustice washed over me.

It was time to look *him* up. I was shocked to find two listings in the directory of his home town, one under his last name and another under a business incorporating his last name. Diligently, I completed searches on both properties and was stunned to discover that Ernest had title to both properties and had carried on a construction business for years. Instead of paying child support, he had obviously stashed his money away to purchase real estate, buy himself a home and start up a lucrative business. And I owned nothing! I was infuriated. I had not received any financial assistance whatsoever from Ernest since Joseph was nine years old.

Although I was filled with anxiety at reopening the old wound, I desperately needed to see that justice was done and, appropriately, filed my application just prior to Father's Day. It had been so many years since I had last spoken to Ernest. No doubt he would have figured he was free and clear long ago.

Ernest was indeed shocked. He got a lawyer. This time, I retained legal counsel. The battle was on. I was finally fighting back.

For months the letters flew back and forth between opposing counsel. Ernest refused to pay the $7,700 owed to me unless he obtained tax relief from Revenue Canada. To his misfortune, Paternity Agreements had never been written into the *Income Tax Act*, and consequently he could not claim the money as a deduction against his income. Through his lawyer, he offered me $5,000 in full and final settlement of all arrears owed to me.

Insufferable, cheap, little worm! He owed me $7,700. Why on earth would I settle for nearly $3,000 less than what I was rightfully entitled to?

Ten torturous months elapsed. Repeated requests were made to Ernest's lawyer to release the monies he was withholding. The ongoing delays caused me unbearable distress and my health deteriorated. It was the same fight all over again. Nothing had changed. I began to wonder if the whole miserable ordeal was worth it.

To my consternation, Ernest's lawyer, Mr. Shade, unexpectedly telephoned me at work. I informed him I was very uncomfortable speaking to him and instructed him to speak to either the Department or my lawyer who was handling the enforcement on my behalf. He ignored my request.

"Maureen, I really want to get this issue resolved. I'm concerned over releasing the money I'm holding in trust to fund any lawsuit you might bring against my client. I want assurances that this will be the end of it." *He was talking to me as if I were a child, but had correctly guessed my intentions. Surely, as a lawyer, he recognized the extent of the injustice and victimization I had suffered and that a lawsuit was inevitable.* Unrelentingly, he continued:

"My client was paying the best he could when he was told he could quit paying child support in 1983. Then out of the blue, he got a rather demanding letter from your solicitor asking for more money. My client feels that coming back and seeking more money was not the right way to proceed. My client says you could have come to him for help."

Who was he kidding? I was infuriated with this man who had no idea of the horrendous struggle and trauma my son and I had endured because of Ernest. None whatsoever. I tried to control the anger in my voice.

"Mr. Shade, it was only after fighting for nine excruciating years with Ernest, attempting to collect a woefully inadequate pittance of $100.00 a month, that I canceled the Paternity Agreement. Payments were in default six to nine months out of every year."

Mr. Shade disputed my claim, and I assured him I had the records to prove it. Again, he brushed me aside.

"Maureen, I agree the amount was peanuts, and my client is of the same opinion. However, my client is not willing to entertain any thought of giving you a cent more than the $7,700."

Where had I heard that expression before—'a cent more'? I was frustrated with this objectionable man who knew so little about his client.

"Mr. Shade, Ernest was the one who set the amount to be paid in the agreement. There was never any input by me, nor was I ever represented by legal counsel. I have paid enormous amounts of money for my son's support, and he currently owes $17,000 in student loans for his Cellular, Molecular, Microbial Biology studies. Do we have the right to deny our children intellectual development if they have talent in that area?" I asked of him.

Amazingly, he conceded, "No, Maureen, we do not."

I then told Mr. Shade that my son would possibly seek his doctorate, but that it would be with further great struggle and cumbersome debt.

"Maureen, is this what started all this?" he asked me. My voice quivered with overwhelming emotion.

"Yes. I have watched my son go through the same struggle I had gone through and saw the cycle repeating itself."

Mr. Shade's voice softened somewhat. "Maureen, wait a minute. I'm going to call Ernest immediately and get right back to you."

Incredibly, only minutes later, Mr. Shade called back with a complete change of attitude.

"Maureen, my client never closed the door on Joseph. He wants Joseph to be a part of his life, and he wants to know him and see him. My client also wants to fund the greater part of his son's education and wants to help his son if he needs it. If my client is paying for his son's education, he should have the privilege of knowing this child."

Why did this all sound so wrong? I was seeking past child support owed to me! Why was this man offering money to fund my son's education instead?

Feeling an escalating, overwhelming anxiety, I wanted nothing more than to terminate the conversation. There was a staunch firmness to my voice as I spoke unwaveringly.

"There are abandonment issues that will not be so easily resolved, Mr. Shade. Contact with Ernest will have to be my son's decision—not Ernest's." He was relentless.

"Maureen, my client wants to help his son, but any forthcoming monies will be in his son's name and not in your name. My client has done very well for himself and is an upstanding member of the community. My client and I do not want any negative publicity getting out about him."

So they were only concerned about negative publicity. Angrily, I retorted:

"Mr. Shade, my son's education is not the real issue, but rather it is the many years I supported my son, putting him through competitive sports to give him a stable, secure life that led up to him entering university. He would not have ended up a microbiology graduate if it were not for my tremendous efforts, and it is for those efforts that I am seeking compensation. I have ended up with nothing. I do not own a home or a business or anything else of value because all my capital has been eroded for twenty years taking care of my son. I want some compensation for that. I would be willing to drop this whole thing if I received a little more than $7,700—enough for a down payment on a home. I have been unjustly forced to bear the burden alone, having paid Ernest's contribution. There should have been joint financial contribution, Mr. Shade." Surprisingly, he agreed with me.

"Your contribution has indeed been immense, and I can assure you that I will see to it that any monies on top of the $7,700 will be in your name and not in your son's name, and I will trust you to dispose of it as you see fit."

How preposterous! He obviously did not know his client— Ernest would never agree to such a proposal. He continued, unabated:

"Maureen, why don't you write a letter addressed to my client and put it in a sealed envelope detailing all expenses you have incurred to date, your son's expenses, as well as your situation to date?"

"Fine," I answered curtly.

"I will give the letter to my client in a sealed envelope, and I will have the monies released within the next day or two."

I hung up the phone. It had been a long, drawn-out, unbearably exhausting eleven months since I had first filed my application. *Was relief finally in sight?* I wondered if this man, Mr. Shade, was truly a man of his word or if I was just being put on hold again.

The following day I dropped by Joseph's apartment to discuss matters with him and made him promise he would not contact Ernest until the issue between Ernest and I had been resolved. Joseph agreed. Satisfied that Joseph would keep his word, I said good-bye and turned to leave.

On my way out, something caught my eye. There were several photographs lying on the stereo, and I stopped to look at them. They were of my son—such a handsome, young man with that beautiful dark hair of his and those thick, dark eyebrows. I gazed at the pictures intently. He was indeed an exceptionally attractive young lad. It was hardly any wonder he often took my breath away ...

An incredible wave of nostalgia flooded over me. I felt an overpowering sensation of wistfulness—a yearning for something—something long ago buried ... lost? Or was it just a forgotten memory? The photographs disturbed me, and I was filled with an unexplainable, deep inner sadness.

Something was wrong. Something was very, very wrong. What was it? The room whirled about me and a dizzying feeling of nausea washed over me. Desperately trying to sound as if nothing was wrong, I spoke with trepidation to my son.

"Joseph, could I borrow these photographs?" He called out from the kitchen.

"Sure, Mom, go ahead! You can have them." Reeling and in shock, I almost ran from his apartment. Thankfully, Joseph was preoccupied and didn't notice the emotional turmoil I was in.

I rushed home with the photographs. Frantically, I tore through bookshelves in the living room, searching for it. *Where the hell was it?* I couldn't find it anywhere and bolted downstairs. Rummaging through old boxes, I scattered things everywhere. *Still no sign of it!* Finally, I ransacked through a pile of old books and found it.

My old high school year book! Anxiously, I fumbled through the pages until I spotted it. *Oh God, there it was—right in front of my eyes.*

Bill. A beautiful picture of Bill. Bill with the dark hair and the thick, dark eyebrows.

Distraught, I ripped through a second year book and found a

picture of Bill's sister. Sure enough, there it was again. *It was all in the eyes and eyebrows—they were unmistakably identical to my son's.*

No, it couldn't be! Oh God, what was happening?

I panicked and began feverishly calling friends. One by one, they each told me I was stressed out and imagining things—that such a thing wasn't possible.

Forget it, Maureen. Put it out of your mind! But the gnawing, unsettling feeling continued to swell like a giant wave about to crush me beneath its massive weight. What was once a tiny, indiscernible voice inside of me shouted, loud and clear:

Maureen, you always wondered if Bill could have been the father of your child! It's time to deal with it! Horrified, I screamed back at the voice:

"No! That was just a fantasy! A silly, foolish fantasy of a naive, young schoolgirl!"

For the next two days I agonized over what to do and met with a close friend, Darcie. Anxiously, I showed her the photographs and year books, and she confirmed my tormented thoughts.

"Can't you see it, Maureen? It's all in the eyes. They're the same!"

Oh God, no! It can't be!!

Joseph was about to reconnect with Ernest—his long-lost father. *What was I supposed to do? As my friends suggested, was I just imagining things because of the stress I had been under? What if Joseph and Ernest met, bonded and somewhere down the line some-one needed a kidney or something. And what if the doctors said some-thing like, 'Oh, and by the way, your son isn't really your son?' What if that happened? Wouldn't that be a worse situation?*

I knew if there was even the slightest possibility that Joseph was not Ernest's son, the truth had to be searched out. Ernest deserved to know if Joseph was not his son. Bill deserved to know if he had a son, and I certainly deserved to know whose child I had had. More important, Joseph had to meet up with the right father.

Oh God, what a mess!

After all our years of interminable fighting, I knew Joseph

would never feel a wholeness, a sense of completeness, until he reconnected with his father. If that was to happen, he had to reconnect with the right father. If I did not have the courage to search out the truth now, it would be impossible to do later and likely would never be done. *Could I live with myself if I neglected to search out the possible existence of a long-buried truth? Could I lie to myself and disregard the incredible awareness that had so powerfully and inexplicably come to me?*

Joseph and Ernest would meet soon for the first time. Would it really make that much difference if that happened just a little sooner?

After agonizing over the whole sordid mess for three days, I finally made a decision. Everything had to be forced out into the open. The truth had to be found out.

It had been five days since I had last spoken with Ernest's lawyer. Monies were about to be paid out. There would never be a better opportunity to deal with this. It was finally time to face the past—to face my worst fear—to face *him.*

Terrified to death, I picked up the phone.

Conscious of my massively heavy, laboured breathing, I nervously dialed the number for Ernest's business. *God help me through this! I screamed silently.*

I knew it was imperative to get Ernest to agree to a DNA paternity test, by whatever means necessary. I would lie if I had to. And I would have to get him to admit that I had been a virgin when it first happened. That was important as well, just in case this all came before a judge.

The phone rang.

"Is Ernest there, please?" I asked nervously.

"Just a minute, please," answered a male voice.

I could hear him yell, "Ernest!" Several seconds went by. My heart pounded furiously, and I felt unbearably distressed.

"Hello?" *Oh God, it was the old, familiar voice—it was him!*

"Ernest?"

"Yeah."

"This is Maureen Lyttle calling."

"Uh huh."

"Ernest, here, here, here's the situation. A small question has arisen in my son's mind and in my mind, and we want conclusive proof that you are in fact his father, so we'd like to ask you to submit to DNA genetics testing at the end of April."

"End of April?"

"Yes."

"Right," he answered.

"My son is writing exams until then, and this would be very traumatic for him. But he wants conclusive proof and, um—so do I."

"Right. Okay."

Carefully, I repeated myself, "The end of April—" He interrupted me.

"You're not sure, eh?" He let out a short chuckle. I was dead silent. There was nothing here to laugh about. Several seconds elapsed. In a very controlled voice, I repeated myself yet again.

"We want conclusive proof, Ernest."

"Okay. Right. Yeah. Okay."

"The end of April. You can let your lawyer know that he can hold on to those funds because I certainly don't want a cent of money should by some incredible miracle some other situation happen to come about from the genetics testing. Okay? It's very doubtful—it's just very doubtful. I think you and I both know that I was in fact a virgin."

"Right." *He admitted it.*

"Okay. I need to clarify this in my son's mind, however, before you jump into his life after eighteen years. Okay? Do you understand that?"

"Yeah."

"Testing is at the Alberta Children's Hospital in Calgary. When my son is finished writing his exams, I will contact you and we will arrange a time when all of us can go down there because we all have to be there at the same time so that I'm not dragging in the wrong kid and you don't substitute in a different person. Okay?"

"Right. Uh huh."

"And that's really why I called."

"Okay," he answered.

"Okay. Bye."

"Real good. Bye."

That was definitely the most civilized conversation we had ever had. The most harrowing and nerve-wracking, but nevertheless the most civilized. I got off the phone and breathed a heavy sigh of relief. I had created doubt. It was out there now—*The Doubt*.

Joseph was furious and refused to agree to a DNA paternity test.

"Mom, Ernie's my father! Listen to me—I'm a microbiologist. I know what I'm talking about. There's no possible way you could have become pregnant—" I was frantic and interrupted him.

"Please, Joseph, please! There may have been a mistake. We have to find out!" He was frustrated and angry with me. I continued to plead with him. I knew we all deserved to know the truth, whatever it was.

"Please, sweetie-pie. I'll pay you to do the test." There was a slight hesitation.

"How much?" he asked.

"One hundred dollars. I'll pay you one hundred dollars cash after the test is done. Is it a deal?" The money was too good to pass up. His voice held a tone of resignation.

"Fine. I'll do the test. But you're wasting your money. I know how the test is going to turn out."

Three more days elapsed. I was tired of the 'con' game being played by Ernest and his lawyer, deliberately withholding the funds from me. In all likelihood, the DNA test would turn out in Ernest's favour, and consequently I sent a scathing letter to the Justice Minister's office detailing the horrific injustice, discrimination and unfairness I had suffered as a single mom under the justice system. I demanded to know why they had failed my son and I for the past twenty years.

A week later a cheque for $7,700 arrived in the mail. Apparently, Mr. Shade had been given an ultimatum by the

Department to pay up or else. They had wanted to take the whole matter back to court. They lost.

Mistakenly, I told Joseph I had received the money, and to my horror, he shouted at me:

"That's my money and I want it! I want it now!"

What on earth was he talking about? I tried to explain that it was money owed to me, not to him, but he refused to listen. For two days he fought ferociously with me over the money, but I paid a few bills and in no time at all it was gone.

Over a month passed and I sent faxes to Ernest, detailing all expenses I had incurred on his son to date. He was furious at the amount of money I had expended and demanded to know what I wanted. I told him:

"Something fair and reasonable." Again he demanded to know exactly what that was, and I replied, "Justice." He was livid.

"The business is family run! My wife is ill in the hospital, and she owns shares in the company. I need her agreement on anything, as well as other family members before any money can be paid out!" Calmly, I replied:

"Ernest, your wife and family are not my concern and not my problem."

"Why the heck do I have to go for a damn DNA test? I have no problem not doing one!"

"Please, Ernest—it's for Joey! Let's just get it over with." He agreed to call me on the following Monday to make arrangements. When he neglected to call, I called him and told him, "9 a.m. Saturday." He was enraged.

"I'm not going to do any damn DNA test! I've talked to my lawyer, and he told me I don't have to do any DNA test until you take me to court!"

"Ernest, you have made Joey wait for twenty-two years—" Angrily, he interrupted me.

"And why was that?"

"Ernest, don't blame me because you abandoned this child eighteen years ago. There is no excuse for abandoning a child. You're a coward, and you're afraid to face your son. I'm not trying to force a reconciliation—" He butted in, fuming.

"I don't want a reconciliation!" His outburst took me by surprise.

"With your son? I don't mean me. I just want to settle the torment in Joey's mind. He deserves peace, and we owe him that much." I could hear the growing resentment in Ernest's voice.

"Isn't your word and my word good enough for him?" he demanded. There was desperation in my voice as I pleaded with him.

"No, it isn't! Look—I will be paying for the whole thing, and I'll pay your gas money to drive to Calgary." Irately, he declined my offer.

"What would you have done if I had died ten years ago?" he shot at me. *I thought: celebrate?*

"Please, Ernest, let's deal with the reality of the situation today—not a hypothetical one. I promise you the procedure will be very quick, and I will be out of your life. There are no legal implications for doing any of this."

Grudgingly, he finally agreed to meet us. I repeated my instructions carefully. "Saturday, May 13 at 9 a.m." I gave him directions to the Alberta Children's Hospital. "Please, Ernest, don't let us down."

Finally, the Big Day arrived. I was feeling horrendous anxiety and distress when I arrived to pick Joey up at 8:40 a.m. He seemed calm and relaxed, while I nervously jumped around like a grasshopper. He was getting perturbed with me.

"Mom, one punch and I could easily kill him," he said. Aghast, I entreated him:

"No, Joseph, please! Don't draw blood until he gives blood." Although part of me wouldn't have minded in the slightest, I made him promise he wouldn't punch Ernest out in the hospital.

We arrived at the Children's Hospital a few minutes early. Nervously, I glanced around but couldn't see *him* anywhere. I hastened to the desk and asked the nurse if Ernest had arrived yet. Suddenly, I heard a voice nearby. "I'm right here." I looked around, and eight feet away there he was—short, skinny and homely-looking. I was shocked and tried to hide my astonishment. Nothing about him was remotely attractive. He had grown a monstrosity of a reddish-coloured mustache that was waxed up into giant curls and covered half his unattractive, thin face. Scrutinizing him, I wondered what I ever saw in such a repulsive, appallingly scrawny-looking, little man. I furtively stole a glance at my tall, dark, exceedingly handsome son and thought to myself: *Yes, indeed, we need to do a DNA test.*

Joseph and I sank into the large, comfortable chairs opposite the admissions desk and tried to relax while Ernest gave his information to the attending nurse. He then approached us and stood there awkwardly, looking like the fool that he always was.

"It's been a long time—what has it been—17-18 years?" *You creep! I wanted to shout at him.* I remained cool, calm, detached.

"Yes, about that. Thank you for coming," I answered in a deadened voice. Ernest replied, "No problem."

I was not about to make him feel comfortable. I was not feeling so generous of spirit on this day, of all days. He continued to stand there, looking ill-at-ease, and finally spoke.

"This must be Joseph." In a toneless voice, I replied:

"Ernest, this is Joseph; Joseph, this is Ernest."

Joseph partially stood up and shook Ernest's hand. Not another word was spoken. I was so very proud of Joseph—he maintained his cool. Marilyn, the co-ordinator, arrived and led us to a quiet sitting area where we sat and asked questions about the testing. I gave her the $150.00 deposit and questioned the technician regarding the type of DNA test they would use, the number of genetic markers searched and so on. I had done my homework. Ernest sat there, hiding behind his big, red, ugly mustache, and said nothing.

We were then led to the lab where they took my blood and a photograph of me first. Then I joined Joseph and watched the nurse take his. Ernest was led to a third room. Anxiously, I stood in the hallway and whispered to the nurse, "I just want to make sure he's actually going to give his blood." The nurse looked at me questioningly and assured me they were getting Ernest's blood. Joseph groaned. "Mom, don't worry. He's not going to back out now."

Yes! I did it! It was all over!

I nearly tore out of the hospital and noticed Joseph lagging behind, lingering, and wondered what the heck he was doing. Then I realized he was curious about Ernest and probably wanted to see more of him. I couldn't get out of the hospital fast enough. Out in the car, I expressed my revulsion at how repulsive Ernest looked. Joey commented that he thought he 'wasn't bad.' I paid Joseph the $100.00 cash, and we enjoyed breakfast at McDonald's.

I felt an overwhelming relief that the DNA test was finally over. There would now be an interminable wait of four to six weeks for the test results. I could only hope and pray that this repugnant, stingy, little man was not Joey's father. There was a 99% chance that Ernest was in fact his father. But there was also the extraordinarily slim possibility that Bill might be Joey's father because of our close sexual contact. It was a very far-reaching possibility, but one that had to be searched out nonetheless. Now it was done. It was all over. It took enormous courage to search out the truth. Nothing was more important now than the truth.

The weeks crept by. I felt inexorably distressed, waiting for the DNA test results. My sleep was extremely disturbed, and I began walking, sometimes several hours a day, in an attempt to relieve the stress. It was useless. On weekends I walked a grueling fifteen miles a day until I ached with fatigue, but incredulously, the stress escalated to horrific proportions the moment I stood still. As the weeks relentlessly slipped by, my health continued to deteriorate, and all I could do was pray fervently to God: *Let the child be Bill's. Let the child be Bill's.* I couldn't imagine what I would do if Ernest were back in my life, through my son. It would be catastrophic, and I knew I would not survive it.

It was July 4, 1995. Independence Day. I had waited nearly two months for the DNA test results. I phoned the hospital and was informed the director was on vacation and would not be back for two weeks. The completed report, as yet unsigned, could therefore not be released to me. I gasped in horror.

The report was there and I couldn't have it because someone was on vacation? How could they fuck with people's lives like this? I knew my health could not take any more. In desperation, I spoke to the chief administrator of the hospital and begged and pleaded with him to make an exception and give me a preliminary report, unsigned.

Marilyn called that same afternoon and informed me she had an interim report ready for me to pick up. I met her at the hospital and we sat opposite each other in a small, private room. I paid her the remaining $700.00 owing for the DNA test and counted out the bills five or six times. Just as she was about to hand me the sheet of paper, I burst into tears.

"Please, I can't handle this here," I begged her. Marilyn hastily slipped the paper into an envelope, sealed it and handed it to me. The stress of the long wait had been too much, and I broke down and wept profusely. I managed to thank Marilyn and left with the DNA paternity test report.

On the drive home, I cried and pleaded to God: *Let it be Bill's child! Let the child be Bill's!* In an attempt to prepare myself for what I knew would be the inevitable, I repeated over and over: *This is Ernest's child. This is Ernest's child. Accept it!*

Finally, I was home. I raced throughout the house, slamming windows, and stood in the kitchen, breathing heavily. Fumbling nervously, I opened the envelope. The sheet of paper listed my name, Joseph's name and the name of the putative father, Ernest. There were a series of strange numbers down the left side of the page and the heading 'shared allele' in a column on the right. Beside each number was a corresponding 'no' under 'shared allele.' The explanatory paragraph at the bottom read:

Seven unlinked loci have been analyzed in the DNA from Maureen Lyttle, Joseph Lyttle and Ernest B. No allele was found to be in common between Joseph Lyttle and Ernest B. at seven of these loci. Ernest B. is, therefore, excluded from being the biological father of Joseph Lyttle.

Signed: R. B. Lowther, M.D., D.Sc., CCMG,
Acting Director, Molecular Diagnostic Laboratory

I screamed in anguish, *Thank you God! Thank you God!* My prayers had been answered. Joseph was in fact Bill's child. I broke the unbelievable news to my son, and he rushed right over. He was in shock as well and promptly got on the phone to the technician at the hospital, querying him about the results of the report. Both of us were stunned. Neither of us knew how to handle the incredible revelation.

Joseph had only one complaint. Dejectedly, he grumbled:

"Mom, I really wanted to be German." I laughed, knowing Bill was of German descent, as was Ernest.

"Sweetie-pie, you still get to be German. Only now you don't get Alzheimer's." We both laughed.

It had been such a long time since I had heard laughter, and it felt good.

I debated giving the money back to Ernest and decided I had rightfully earned it after all that he had put me through. He would get his copy of the official report in two weeks and would finally know the truth for himself. Meanwhile, I could relax.

The next day I purchased two dozen white roses and dropped them off for Marilyn with my sincere thanks.

9   *Revelation*

Joseph graduated with a degree in Cellular, Molecular, Microbial Biology. I had not yet reconciled with my mother, and when I caught a glimpse of her with my two sisters at my son's graduation, I could not bear to acknowledge them and sat by myself. I met my son afterwards and took him and his girlfriend out for dinner. Joseph then left, telling me he was going out with friends.

He lied. Instead, he went over to my sister Josephine's for a graduation party in his honour. My family was all there. My sister had not asked me if I minded her hosting a grad party for my son, nor was I invited to attend. It was a day I desperately needed to share with my son, and once again, they succeeded in destroying something very special and important to me. I was crushed by Josephine's cruelty and other than leaving a vulgar message of, '*Go straight to fucking hell!*' on her answering machine, I had no desire to speak to her again. I had put up with fifteen years of her contempt and abuse and had had enough.

I went for a long walk and cried tearfully for hours. As I passed over the Crowchild Trail overpass, I glanced down at the six lanes of fast-moving traffic below and wondered what it would be like to climb over the guard rail and jump to my death. Horrified at my self-destructive thoughts, I gripped the railing and hastened from the bridge. For the next two days I felt a powerful urge to return and each time my thoughts turned to jumping into the traffic seventy-five feet below.

Knowing that I could not trust myself, I stumbled from the bridge for the last time and did not return. It was simply too dangerous.

I felt as if I were in the middle of the ocean, struggling to stay afloat. The waves kept crashing down hard on me again and again. I was struggling to breathe; I was fighting to survive. I was drowning and there was no one to save me.

The call finally came. The DNA paternity report was official.

The diagnostic laboratory had discovered additional unshared alleles (genes), effectuating an even stronger report. I spoke to a geneticist, and he informed me that I could be very confident that the report was not only reliable, but also indisputable.

It was a nerve-wracking day as I drove frantically to the hospital on my lunch hour to pick up the DNA report and rushed back to work. That afternoon, I couriered a photograph of Joseph, together with a burdensome and laborious letter that had taken me two weeks to compose, to Bill in Vancouver. The letter read:

Dear Bill:

This is by far the most difficult letter I have ever had to write.

I hope you remember me. I went to St. Mary's High School in 1970-1972. I gave birth to a child in October of 1972.

On May 13, 1995, DNA paternity testing was completed with my son's putative father, whom I had not seen nor heard from for the past eighteen years. The paternity test report, completed by the Alberta Children's Hospital in Calgary, indicates there were no shared alleles (genes) in common between my son and the putative father [Ernest], and the putative father has therefore been excluded from being my son's biological father.

The only other man I had any sort of close contact with at that particular time was you, Bill, three weeks prior to losing my virginity to the putative father. I had always assumed that I had conceived through the latter incident, unaware at that time that conception could occur through close contact. The DNA report, however, substantiates that this is in fact what happened. Needless to say, this has been a shocking revelation after all these years. If you would like to see the DNA report, I will certainly make it accessible to you.

Please be assured that I am not asking for anything from you, Bill. Under the circumstances, I felt you had the right to know. If you wish to do further DNA testing with my son and I, we would unquestionably and happily agree to it.

My son is a wonderful, intelligent, young man who graduated in June from the University of Calgary with a degree in Cellular, Molecular, Microbial Biology. He will most likely continue doctorate studies to obtain his Masters in CMMBI. I have attached a photograph of Joseph for you.

Bill, if you would like to talk (and I most genuinely hope you do), please do not hesitate to contact me at home at [phone no.]

Sincerely,

Maureen Lyttle

The package was on its way. Tomorrow Bill would get the news. It was extremely difficult to concentrate at work, thinking about what might happen and how Bill would react.

The following day, the courier company informed me the package had been delivered into the recipient's mailbox at 11:52 a.m. *It was done.* I felt mixed relief and apprehension and was physically drained and exhausted when I finally got home from work. I kept repeating to myself: *He won't phone, Maureen. You've done your job. Now sit down and relax—it's over.*

I wasn't home more than ten minutes when the phone rang. Tentatively, I picked it up.

"Maureen, this is Bill." Shocked to hear his voice, I gasped and managed to utter, "Oh God!" Bill's voice brimmed with excitement.

"Maureen, I got your letter and didn't know whether to laugh, cry or lie down. I took the picture to work and showed a guy who asked me, '*Who's that—your brother?*'" I was astounded.

"Bill, he reminds me of John, your brother."

"Maureen, he's a *Lentz*! I don't have to look any further than the damn picture. He has the *Lentz* look. It's in the eyes and the eyebrows. Don't you see it?" I was overcome with emotion. *He saw it too.*

"Bill, I had forgotten what you looked like. All I have is a tiny picture of you in a yearbook." Amazingly, Bill sounded so positive, so confident and so very self-assured.

"Maureen, I look like your son," he replied fervently. I was overjoyed to hear Bill's voice after so many years.

"I never thought you would call, Bill."

"Why wouldn't I call?"

"Ernest never bothered with Joseph, and we're used to abandonment and rejection. We're used to being alone out here. Why should I expect anything different from you?"

"Maureen, you're not alone anymore. I'm right here. And I'm very, very proud of what you've done. It must have taken a lot of courage."

"It's so good to hear you say that, Bill." His words touched my soul and I wept silently.

"Bill, do you have a wife or a family? Will they be okay with this?"

"Don't worry about that, Maureen. I have a girlfriend and she's wonderful. She'll be really great with this."

How was it that Bill was dealing with such a difficult situation with apparent ease? Why was I feeling a little skeptical—a little apprehensive?

"How is it that you're taking this so well, and I'm taking this so hard?" I asked him uneasily.

"Maureen, you've been with him and worked hard to raise him." I was still confused.

"No, Bill, I mean why is this so hard on me emotionally? Perhaps it's because I have had to face the trauma of the past." I told him about the miserable life I had had with Ernest, the drug dealing and how I had been terrified that I would be taken away and Joey snatched from me. I told Bill that when the abusive relationship with Ernest ended, I was traumatized for many years and finally got down to the business of raising my son.

"That's good."

"I did a good job, Bill."

"I can see that," he answered reassuringly.

"Bill, I've been in such a terrible denial for so many years. I couldn't face the past until very recently, and finally I saw the resemblance of Joseph to you and said to myself: *There's been a big mistake.* That little, indiscernible voice inside of me that was once a whisper became a scream, and I knew I had to do the DNA test with Ernest."

Passionately, Bill proclaimed, "Maureen, I've never been married or had children of my own—I always wanted a boy. I feel like I should be handing out cigars." I was filled with immense pride, hearing those words uttered from Bill, the father of my son.

"Well, Bill, you've got your boy. He's not in diapers—he's a young man now."

"Maureen, he's only twenty-two."

"Yes, you're right."

"It's too bad we didn't know this twenty-two years ago," Bill said sadly. I sighed heavily.

"Yes, it is, but twenty-two years ago, a blood test would have been inconclusive, and they didn't have DNA paternity tests." I mentioned to Bill that perhaps we should do such a test.

"Maureen, you just tell me what you want me to do, and I'll do it."

I felt deliriously happy. We talked further about how and where it happened, and although Bill said he didn't remember the incident, he did remember that we used to sneak off clandestinely together. I told him if he remembered that much, it would have to be good enough for me. I explained to Bill that I had had a virgin birth, and Bill chuckled.

"I must have had motile sperm."

We discussed his schedule and getting together for a reunion. He explained he was busy for the next few weeks.

"We've waited twenty-two years, Bill. Another few weeks won't matter." Bill insisted we needed to get this done as soon as possible because his father was dying and he wanted Joseph to meet him before he died.

"Maureen, August 24 or 25 would be a good time for me." I was walking on air.

"You mean I'm actually going to see you again after all these years?" I asked in disbelief. Bill laughed.

"You bet!"

We said good-bye. I sat down and wept tears of joy. So many years had gone by, yet in a few short moments, the past had miraculously become the present. And Bill was so pleased to have a son. Nothing could have brought me more happiness. Joseph was going to have a father, and I was going to see Bill—the father of my child. It was too good to be true.

I was right. It was indeed too good to be true.

Over a week passed. Reality hit me like a nuclear blast. Thank God Alice came along while I was on the mall at lunch hour. I told her my story and how I felt I wasn't good enough to be the mother of Bill's child. She chided me gently.

"Of course you're worthy. For all you know this guy's a jerk. Get him off that magical pedestal. It'll be a year before you know what kind of a guy Bill really is." I told Alice about Ernest being forced to pay $7,700 and that he had probably spent an additional $3,000 in legal fees fighting it. She laughed.

"See, Maureen—God does have a sense of humour." Through my tears, I managed to smile weakly. Perhaps Alice was right. Perhaps God did have a sense of humour.

That evening I went for a late night walk in the moonlight and found myself at the playground in the park. I lay down on the children's slide and gazed up at a beautiful night sky filled with twinkling stars. My eyes clouded with tears, and I prayed fervently for peace to come to me.

Initially elated at the shocking news of my son's paternity, I was now sick with grief and guilt. Joseph could have had a father all those years had I known. I regretted the past horrors with Ernest, which I never would have had to endure had I known the truth. I was confused as to my own identity. After all, if I wasn't the mother of Ernest's child, who was I? My son's identity confused me as well, and I was not able to fully recognize Joseph as my own child. The distressing realization filled me with unspeakable despair.

I would come to realize, in time, that I had suffered a painful identity crisis, not only of myself, but also with regard to my son. It explained why I had often stared at Joseph in restaurants and elsewhere, perplexed as to his good looks and much to Joseph's chagrin. So many times I would watch him approach from a distance, and the sight of him would take my breath away. Through the years, I had watched for signs of Ernest in his face, but there had been none. Indeed, I had always thought the gods had shone favorably down upon me in giving me such a beautiful child, even though there was always something about my son that I never fully understood and had been unable to identify, so deeply buried was it in my subconscious. Finally, by the grace of God, my eyes had opened and I could see.

Two weeks passed and I knew it was the day Ernest would be in possession of the DNA report. To calm myself, I lay outside in the backyard, soaking up the sun. The warm rays felt soothing on my tired, weary body. Squirrels scampered through the trees, playfully fighting over the seeds I had scattered about. I heard the sound of a broken twig and leapt off the lawn chair in terror.

It was Ernest! He had a gun, and he was going to kill me! Oh God, it was only a squirrel! My nerves were completely shattered, my mind and body overfatigued. Every sound—every subtle movement—startled me and caused me to gasp in alarm. I could not lay outside in the warm sunshine and instead locked myself inside the house where I felt safe.

Several days later I received a letter from Mr. Shade asking what I had done with the money and perhaps it was still in my possession. *Oh God, was this never going to end?* Briskly, I informed Mr. Shade the money that had been owed by his client pursuant to a Paternity Agreement dating back to 1975 had been depleted, and I was therefore considering the matter closed. I mailed the letter and hoped to God that that would be the end of it.

I never heard from Ernest or his lawyer again.

I spoke to Joseph that evening. He sounded hurt, and I assured him he had a right to his feelings and emotions, whatever they were. He told me that he didn't want to see Bill or have anything to do with him and said dejectedly:

"Mom, I've never had a father in my life—why the hell would

I need one now?" I tried to comfort him and told him to try not to blame Bill, that it was not Bill's fault, nor was it my fault—that sometimes there's just no one to blame.

"Heck, Bill doesn't even remember being with me. How do you think that makes me feel? I guess the joke's on me." I paused reflectively. "If you don't want to see Bill, don't worry, you don't have to." Joey said he was just sick of all 'this shit.' Frankly, I didn't blame him. So was I.

I knew I needed to see Bill one more time for closure. I needed to see the man whose child I had unknowingly conceived—the man who resembled my son. I needed to see the father of my son to make everything real.

I woke up the following morning laughing from a dream I was having. There were hundreds of adults on a lawn, all dressed as little children. Even men dressed as little girls, wearing wigs with ringlets. Everyone was laughing. I found it humorous, but I was baffled as to what it all meant. I remembered running down a path to get there in time, losing my shoes in the process. Later, I reflected on the dream, and I knew I was finally in touch with the playful, little child within me that had been lost for so long.

It was August 24, the day Bill said he would arrive for a reunion. He had sounded so sincere and I had gullibly believed his every word. I could not help thinking that having been a young girl of seventeen who handled an unexpected and traumatic pregnancy alone, surely Bill, a grown man of forty-three, could handle it now. *Why was he treating me like this?* I was bewildered by Bill's cruel, contradictory behaviour and sat in the park again that evening. My grief was unbearable.

Joseph and I had survived up until now without Bill, and we would continue to do so. I didn't know what to tell my son. Being abandoned by one father must have been a painful disappointment for him. What would abandonment by two fathers do to him?

The weekend was over, and Bill never bothered to call as he had promised.

Several times I caught myself lying in bed feeling sick, tired and depressed and forced myself to get up. Perhaps Bill wasn't worthy after all. And how foolish of me to have thought that I wasn't worthy of being the mother of his child. Hadn't I single-handedly raised his son and been a loving, nurturing mother to him all those years?

I took Joseph to Earl's for dinner and told him that Bill had not called as he had promised, that he probably couldn't handle any of this and that we should just do the best to get on with our lives. Joey agreed with me.

"Mom, I haven't lost anything." *What a brave thing for him to say.* I was filled with a deep love and compassion for my son.

"No, my son, you haven't lost anything, but we have gained something—the truth. They know you're alive, and they know you exist. The truth cannot be denied or buried any longer. It's out in the open—they know you're here. Joseph, we have a lot of courage—something not everyone has."

Joseph acted cocky throughout dinner, and I knew he was still hurting and merely trying to justify his existence.

The months slipped by. I felt a deep sadness at Bill's inability to handle the situation. I had gone through incredible suffering to search out the truth for all of us, and Bill had left us hanging in the end. I was heartbroken.

The fighting with Joseph continued and I was at my wits' end. Finally, a realization hit me and I sent Joseph an e-mail.

Joseph, I believe you have been taking out all your unresolved anger and feelings regarding abandonment and rejection on me. I did not abandon you, nor did I reject you. I have always been there for you. But I cannot take your anger anymore. You owe me respect. It's time you took responsibility for your own life and quit blaming me. You have a right to feel hurt, but you do not have the right to take your anger out on me.

Joseph didn't bother replying.

Seven months had passed since I first contacted Bill, and it was time to speak to my mother. After much deliberation and soul-searching, I decided to get things out in the open with her and express how I felt. It had been bothering me for some time that if she passed away, I would be left with a lot of unresolved issues that I had never addressed with her. I felt I owed it not only to myself, but also to her, to explain why I had not been in her life.

I phoned Mom and told her I had had a very painful year and a half and confided to her the issue regarding my son's paternity and that Ernest was not my son's father. To my astonishment, she asked:

"Is the father's name Bill? Bill Lentz?" I was completely taken aback by her divulgence and asked her how she possibly knew that. Before she could respond, I knew the answer.

"Was I drunk?" I asked her warily.

"Yes, you were."

Oh God, it had to have been the night of my son's third birthday party. I had been appallingly intoxicated and had wept hysterically to my mother. The next morning I remembered feeling very uncomfortable and unable to recall anything I had said to her the previous evening.

I was embarrassed and perturbed by mother's admission. All those years she had known of my subconscious inner turmoil and never once alluded to it or breathed a word of it to me. And the turmoil had remained deeply buried in my subconscious. But mother had always secretly known.

I stressed to her that my son's paternity did not impact on her life or on anyone else's life and that it was not a topic for open discussion. She agreed that it was no one's concern. I told her Ernest was bound by law to pay the money to me and that I did not, by law, have to repay it. She was indeed surprised.

"Mom, I've been in therapy, and I have had to go back to the past to deal with very painful memories. I have been hurt badly by several members of the family, and I realize I have the right to make choices. I have the right to choose to have those in my life who love and respect me, and the right to choose not to have those in my life who cannot give me that respect. Joe and Josephine have caused me great pain and suffering, and I never want them in my life again."

To my amazement, mother denied knowing what they had done. I persisted.

"Mom, Josephine continually overstepped my boundaries and undermined the relationship between my son and I. None of you ever recognized my son and I as a family unit, and Joseph and I had the right to be a family, separate and apart from all of you. Having family dinners where I was the only one specifically excluded and where my son was invited behind my back were acts of cruelty, not of love." Undaunted, I continued:

"Mom, this has always been a very dysfunctional family that has never dealt with issues. Emotions have always been suppressed and denied and we were never a healthy, loving family, dating back to when I was young and living at home." Then I hit her with the most painful of truths.

"Mom, I never really felt your love but only felt your sadness over the years." She was shocked and distressed and emphatically denied everything.

"I loved you all so very much when you were little! I was always happy, and I was never sad. Things fell apart when you became teenagers and laughed and made fun of me for being old-fashioned and not very smart. I tried to get you help, but you refused to go."

Did she not realize that she needed help? And what was this 'I loved you all so very much when you were little'? Did that mean she stopped loving us when we were older? Could she only love us as babies?

"Mom, if it was too painful for me to deal with at that time, you must stop blaming me—I was only a sixteen-year-old kid."

"Maureen, you're imagining everything! We were indeed a happy family!"

"Mom, I'm not imagining anything at all. I remember things very clearly."

She was extremely upset that I felt she never loved me and told me that I was loved more than anyone. I didn't argue but repeated that I never felt that love—only her sadness.

I told her I had read a lot of psychology books, and she became angry.

"Psychology is not the answer!" I was adamant and told her it most certainly was, especially in dysfunctional families.

"Mom, our relationship has always been unhealthy because all we ever talk about is me or my son. We never talk about you. I really know nothing about you or your life."

Mom vehemently denied knowing what I was talking about. There was anxiety and irritation in her voice.

"What's there to know? I lived on the farm, then with your father. That's all there is to know!"

Undeterred by her anger, I remarked dryly, "So mother, you can sum up your whole life in just one sentence." Her voice was bitter and resentful.

"Ask me anything—I'll tell you!"

"Mom, anytime I ever ask you anything, you shut down and your defenses go up."

"That's not true! I don't understand what you're talking about." I gently reminded her of the letter she wrote to me saying that all her memories were too painful to talk about. I told her that she had a wall around her that no one could penetrate and that I was tired of trying. I could hear the fury rising in her voice.

"I don't have a wall around me! I feel sick and I have to get off this phone! I don't want to hear any more!" No longer under her restraint, I asked her point-blank:

"Was my father an alcoholic?" She gasped in alarm.

"He would only have a few drinks!" I persisted.

"But he drank all the time." She was livid and denied that he was an alcoholic and demanded to know where I had gotten my information from. I didn't press the issue further. It was time to hold her accountable for all the toxic shame she had so unjustly burdened me with.

"Mom, do you remember calling me a slut and ripping up my birth control prescription when I was young?" She was horrified.

"Maureen! Where do you get that from? I did no such thing!" Straightforwardly, I told her that she did and reminded her that sexual issues were a subject that she was never able to discuss with us. She relented and agreed sex was never discussed. I let it go.

"Mom, this family has never dealt with issues, and it has never been a healthy, loving family."

"I know what you're trying to say! You're insinuating there was hanky panky going on. I can tell you there was no hanky panky going on." Patiently, I told her I was insinuating no such thing.

"I know what this is about! This is because I was pregnant before I got married. That's what this is all about." I again calmly told her that that had nothing to do with it. I explained that the family did things to deliberately hurt one another and that it was very dysfunctional and that if I did not get respect from her or the rest of them, they would no longer be in my life. She was shocked and angry and insisted on getting off the phone. As she now knew where I stood, I let her do just that.

Her control over me was over. I was free at last. And it only took forty-two long, torturous years. I would never allow anyone to blame me again for being a sixteen-year-old child who found counseling too painful. Mother needed help long before I could ever be helped. I did not cause my family's dysfunction. But I was now free of it.

The conversation with mother was on Sunday. On Monday evening when I arrived home from work, there was a nasty, disturbing message on my answering machine from my older brother Brian.

Maureen, a few weeks ago you told me I had to have respect for your feelings. Well, I just received some stunning news, and I'm just wondering where those standards were when you went after Ernest for money you knew you were not rightfully entitled to since he was not the father of Joey. I really don't know what else to say—I'm so stunned by the news and all the high-toned talk that you gave me. But I'll always remember—about feelings and how much regard you had for his and his wife's feelings. Bye.

Astounded, I phoned Brian and tried to tell him it was none of his business. He refused to let me speak, laughed a dirty-sounding laugh and hung up. I phoned back and yelled three words to him:

"Fuck off, Brian!" and slammed down the phone. Immediately, I telephoned Mom and angrily confronted her.

"It's too bad you didn't tell Brian that the DNA test was done three months after the monies were paid to me! It's also too bad you didn't tell Brian that by law the money was owed to me by Ernest as the legal father of my son. It's really too bad you don't know the law, mother!"

I didn't get a chance to utter another word. She, too, had hung up on me.

Brian was angry that I had called him on his inability to respect my feelings or emotions in a talk we had had a month previous. This was his way of getting even and knocking me back down to size. Sadly, I could not have imagined a more cruel thing he could have done.

I began to weep uncontrollably and slumped to the floor in excruciating pain. Suddenly and inexplicably, I heard a powerful, commanding voice. *Forgive them, Maureen, for they know not what they do.* Immediately, the pain ceased; the tears stopped. They were too unhealthy, and they did not know what they were doing.

Awareness had not yet come to any of them.

10   *The Betrayal*

Three more months elapsed. It was now April of 1996. I spoke to a social worker at an adoption agency and told her my story and how my health had deteriorated since I had been left hanging by the birth father nine months after a conversation with him.

"Why on earth haven't you called him?" she asked incredulously.

"I was afraid to," I answered.

"Maureen, you will never feel a sense of closure or resolution until you get an answer. He owes you that much." *Of course she was right. It was the least Bill could do.*

"How would you feel if that answer was 'No'?" she asked me gently.

"It would be okay—I just need an answer one way or another. I can't seem to let go or get on with my life without an answer." She agreed with me and told me to take the bull by the horns and write to Bill. I thanked her and hung up.

Bill had forced me to wait nine long, torturous months, and I could not wait any longer. I decided it was time to call him and dialed his number. The operator's message rang in my ears. *The number you have reached is out of service.*

Oh God, Bill was gone! He was running! I panicked.

I phoned Joseph and told him that Bill was gone and there was no forwarding phone number for him. The sadness was unmistakable in my son's voice and my heart ached for him. This had been so difficult on both of us. We spoke for a few minutes and I hung up.

I felt sick to my stomach. *Perhaps I could get ahold of one of Bill's family living in the city and relay a message to Bill.* Feverishly, I began calling various numbers and reached a lodge and then a nursing home. The operator gave me an address, and mistakenly thinking it was Bill's mother's address, I dashed out of the house and drove in a frenzy to the address the operator had given me.

To my shock and dismay, the address was that of the Colonel Belcher Hospital. *There must be some mistake.* I got out of the car, checked and rechecked the address and finally got up the courage to enter the hospital through the side door. I spoke to the night watchman and he confirmed there was a Mr. Lentz [Bill's father] there and that he was ill. He asked me who I was. I told him I wouldn't bother Mr. Lentz and left. Back in the car, I sat and wept profoundly. *How I would have loved to have met my son's grandfather. Perhaps I would have finally recognized and understood my son's identity.*

Sadly, it was not to be. I knew I could not go barging up there to poor Mr. Lentz's hospital room. I had to go through Bill. Sick with grief, I drove home, weeping in terrible distress.

The panic had escalated to horrendous proportions by the time I got home. Once again, I began frantically dialing phone number after phone number and finally succeeded in reaching Bill's sister, Linda. I told her I was an old classmate of her brother's, and without hesitation, she gave me Bill's phone number and informed me that Bill had moved in with his girlfriend in December. Grateful for the information, I thanked her and hung up. Summoning all the courage I could, I bravely dialed Bill's new number. Thankfully, he answered the phone. My voice quivered with heartbreaking emotion.

"Bill, I need you to tell me right now that you do not want your son in your life so that I can get on with my life. There has been no resolution to any of this—no sense of closure—and I need that so I can get on with my life." There was a deafening pause.

"Well, no, I can't." In desperation, I pleaded with him.

"Please, Bill, it's been nine long months, and I really need to hear that from you right now so that I can move forward and put this all behind me." There was unmistakable anger and resentment in Bill's voice.

"You don't understand! My attorney told me not to speak to you or admit to anything. He said if I stepped foot in Alberta, the second I got off the plane, you could slap me with a subpoena to appear in court for a DNA test, and you could ruin me financially." I was floored and gasped in astonishment.

"Subpoena?"

"Yes! They could stick a needle in my arm and get my blood, and they could force me to pay twenty years of child support. My lawyer told me I could be dragged back and forth to Alberta, and you could devastate me financially." *I couldn't believe what I was hearing. Hadn't I made it clear I only wanted closure?* I managed to laugh weakly.

"Okay, Bill, now we're getting somewhere. I wish you would have told me this before. I can deal with your fears, Bill, but only if you tell me what they are. This was never, ever about money." He was furious.

"What is it about?" he demanded.

I answered him candidly, "This was about truth, Bill."

Stubbornly, he persisted. "What do you want?"

"Bill, I was hoping you might want to see your son, that's all. This was just never about money."

"You say that now—what about later?" he lashed back. I was confused.

"Bill, you haven't been in your son's life for the past twenty-three years. How could I, in all consciousness, ask you for money now? My son is grown—I raised him. It's done and it's too late to talk about money."

He went on, grumbling about his attorneys looking after his interests and that he had made bad decisions in the past and that's what his attorneys were for. I told him matter-of-factly that I had worked for lawyers for the past eighteen years and that if this had been about money, I would have been out to B.C. a long time ago to take this to court. Grudgingly, he agreed.

"Well, yeah, I guess you could have." He paused. "I'll have to face what I've done." I was silent. Bill continued obstinately, "I'll have to change my life." Perplexed, I asked him:

"Why? Because you're a parent and you'd have to commit to your son?"

"No! I'd have to look at where I've been and where I'm going." I thought: *Big deal. Isn't that life?*

"My lawyer wanted to know—didn't you have any inclination?"

"Well, yes, when he started to turn into a Bill Lentz." Bill chuckled. Almost apologetically, I explained:

"Bill, I didn't know what you looked like growing up. I didn't see it until Joseph got to the age you were when I met you. I was a very naive seventeen-year-old. I kept thinking: *Bill would know. Bill would know if he got me pregnant.* But it was just a very naive seventeen-year-old's way of thinking." Bill was strangely silent.

"Bill, why don't you ask your lawyer—" He interrupted me impatiently.

"Forget about the lawyer! There's no reason why Joseph can't meet his family out there. My mother is on the Island and will be here on Saturday. I'm going to give her your number, and you, Joseph and my sister can get together for tea. I'll let my mother judge your character. She'll be able to tell what you're like, and she'll know immediately if Joseph is my son."

Judge my character? I told Bill fine, we'd leave it up to his mother.

"I want to see Joseph, but when I do, I would like it to be on neutral ground out here in B.C." *How on earth was that neutral ground? I wondered.*

"Bill, that's fine with me. Do you want Joseph to go alone?"

"No, you can come with him." Relieved to hear that I could be at the reunion, I replied firmly:

"Good, he'll need my support."

It was time to confront Bill.

"You left me hanging last July, and that really hurt, Bill. Joseph and I were both very hurt by that. It was like being left dangling over a cliff. We're both trying to heal from that pain, but I won't put Joseph through that again until the meeting is a sure thing. Joseph was devastated that you didn't call back last July, Bill. He felt you had rejected him."

"Maureen, I didn't have your number."

"Bill, it was on the letter I sent you."

"No, it wasn't."

"I'm listed in the directory," I insisted.

"I guess I could have looked your number up. I thought you were supposed to call me," he said resignedly.

"No, Bill, you specifically said you would call back. I won't tell Joseph about the meeting because of what happened last July."

"Fine! Don't tell him about any of this until my mother calls." I agreed to Bill's request and hung up.

A week passed and there was no phone call from Bill.

I came home from work exhausted, and needing to see my son, I asked Joseph to join me for dinner. We went to Earl's and ordered a lovely meal of chicken wings, chicken tenders and pizza. Joseph was distracted. It was obvious he had something on his mind.

"Mom, I was out playing golf with Brian's dad, and he said it would be a good idea to write to Bill. Mom, I want to write to him, but how can I if we don't know where he lives?" Seeing that he was worried, I spoke up.

"Joseph, I have a confession to make—I know where Bill is." Joseph stared at me, surprised. I explained:

"Joseph, I spoke to Bill last week. His mother was supposed to call me by today to arrange a meeting with you, me and his sister. But she didn't call. I've done everything I can possibly do. I'm going to give you the phone numbers and let you handle this. So what if you make a mistake? Dust yourself off, get up and start again."

We continued talking, and I mentioned to Joseph that I had forgiven Bill for any monies he may have owed me. To my dismay, Joseph grumbled that Bill still owed him for university. I became angry and reproached him.

"Bill owes you nothing! He hasn't been in your life all these years—he doesn't owe you anything." Joseph adamantly disagreed. I didn't bother to argue with him. There was no sense because Joseph didn't understand the law as I did.

"Joseph, I believe Bill was frightened by what his lawyer told him, and that's probably why we haven't heard from him for the past nine months. We cannot let this go without some kind of resolution, one way or another." It was a peaceful supper, and we left for home to make the call.

Joseph nervously dialed Bill's sister's number, and they spoke for several minutes. I heard him say at one point, "Well, no, I was nervous about going that route. But then, I'm nervous going this route." Linda confirmed she would call back to arrange a meeting for Friday morning.

Joseph still held the paper in his hand and, to my amazement, continued dialing.

"What are you doing?"

"Fuck it, Mom! I'm calling Bill." I gasped in astonishment, held my head in my hands, groaned and escaped to the living room.

The conversation with Bill lasted less than a minute. At one point I heard Joseph say, "So how are you doing, Big Guy?" I chuckled and felt incredibly proud of my son. He got off the phone, and incredulous, I asked him:

"What happened?" Joseph said Bill was feeding two kids and would phone him back in half an hour. I drove Joseph home and told him to call me if he heard from Bill.

I waited anxiously for Joseph to phone me that evening, but there was no call. Weary and worried about my son, I drove over to his house, and his roommate reassured me everything was fine and that Joseph had gone out drinking with his friends. I felt a wave of relief, knowing that everything was probably all right.

The following day Joseph told me Bill had called him back as promised. Apparently, Bill told Joseph if he wanted to come and stay with him out in Vancouver, that would be fine. As well, if Joseph wanted to go to the University of British Columbia for environmental studies, Bill had promised that he would do what he could to help, and that if Joseph needed money, to call him.

"What did you say to Bill that Bill would offer you money?" Joseph was furious at my inference. I was undeterred by his feigned indignation.

"Joseph, I had to forgive a big debt. Can't you forgive whatever perceived debt you feel Bill owes you?"

"How could you think such a thing? You don't know me very well if you think so low of me. How could you think I wanted any money from Bill when he hasn't been in my life all these years?" *Why did his words sound so familiar?*

It was April 19—the Big Day. No one had bothered to call to invite me to the meeting with Bill's family. I was heartbroken. I had fervently hoped that I would have been invited to the meeting to meet these people who were related to my son. At noon, the phone rang. It was Joseph. He was extremely agitated.

"Mom, I'm scared. I don't want to go through with this." I spoke compassionately to him.

"Joseph, you want to run, don't you?"

"Yes, I do," he answered.

"Are you alone?"

"Yes, I am." I was angry.

"Joseph, you should not be going through this alone! You should have had support at the meeting and it's very wrong that they did not invite me to be there with you to give you that support. I knew this was going to be hard on you—that's why I wanted to be there for you. Joseph, just feel the fear and jump in. I will be right there with you. It's too late to run. If you get really scared, tell them you have to call me, and I'll calm you down."

I got off the phone and prayed that my son would get through the meeting okay. He was absolutely terrified and all alone. My heart broke and I felt so very, very sad for him.

Two hours later, exhausted from a lack of sleep, I decided that Joseph must have gotten through the meeting with Bill's family and wearily crawled into bed. I was about to nod off when there was a sudden, loud banging at the door. It was Joseph. He was obviously distressed.

"How did the meeting go? Did your grandma give you a big hug and kiss?" I asked him.

"No," he answered, rather dejectedly.

"I guess this wasn't a *Welcome to the family meeting*, but rather it was a *Let's see if you are family meeting*," I responded.

Joseph was not impressed and said it was really uncomfortable.

"Mom, I'm like them." We sat and talked and he gloomily handed me a picture and remarked ruefully, "I don't think I look like this dude." I stared at the photograph. It was of Bill, apparently taken several years earlier. I marveled at it. It was indeed Bill—the father of my son.

"Oh, isn't he a handsome man? You have his eyes and eyebrows!" I exclaimed elatedly. Joseph would not be persuaded. I was unable to put the picture down and asked Joseph if I could make a copy of it right away. After grumbling for a while, he finally relented.

I felt uncomfortable upon hearing they had questioned Joseph about Ernest and I. Joseph was just a baby at the time and had no recollection whatsoever of Ernest.

Bill's brother Michael was at the meeting and told my son he worked with a girl who used to hang out with me in high school. Michael told Joseph she used to know me and had a picture of Joseph when he was a baby. Michael had gotten the picture from her and had given it to his mother, who then brought the picture to Bill in Vancouver. Bill had recognized the baby picture and said, "That's me!" His mother had corrected him with, "No, that's Joey."

A few days later I called Joseph to see if he was okay. He was still grumbling and wanted me to buy him a coat, and feeling sorry for him, I agreed. I told him he deserved something special after what he had been through. On the drive to Chinook Centre, he became very upset.

"I'm angry at you—it's all your fault!" I was upset as well.

"How could I possibly have known at seventeen years of age

that this could have happened?" I retaliated.

"Mom, it's easier to keep on hating Ernest than to deal with the fact that someone actually wants me!"

"Joseph, you have to let go of your hate for Ernest. Until you do, you won't be able to have any love for Bill." He was furious and resentful.

"Mom, I could have had a father all these years!"

"Maybe not," I replied dubiously.

"No, Mom. This is a good family. They all talk and listen to one another."

"Good. They were open. That's what a family is supposed to be like."

We visited a couple of stores in pursuit of a coat, and Joseph remained dejected all day. "What's the point? They're strangers to me."

I grabbed him and shook him. "You have a father who wants you. You have a family who wants you. Don't give me any more of this self-pitying crap." I hugged him tightly.

Six days passed without a phone call from the Lentz's or from Bill. I was extremely disappointed with all of them, particularly Bill. He could at least have called his son and asked him how the meeting went with his family. Nothing. I was not impressed. Nor did Bill bother to call me.

Nearly two more weeks elapsed without any further word from Bill. I told Joseph that Bill had told me all kinds of wonderful things on the phone and had done the same thing to me last July when he left me hanging.

"Bill says what you want to hear, and he cannot follow through. We have to get on with our lives," I urged Joseph. "Bill is terrified of commitment and probably cannot handle this. He does not have the courage you and I do. He is a coward, and you are a far better man than Bill could ever hope to be. I'm very disappointed that Bill didn't at least call you to ask how the meeting went with his family." Joseph wasn't listening to me. It appeared he had his own agenda.

"Mom, I want to go to UBC and live in Richmond." *Where Bill lives?*

"Joe, if you want to go because Bill is there, it would be a big mistake."

"No, Mom, that's not why," he maintained.

"Joseph, you'll never have Bill to yourself. You'll have to share him with his girlfriend and her three children, and if you live with Bill, there could be a lot of jealousy and a lot of people living in one house. How could you have quiet study time?" Joseph assured me he would not live with Bill, but rather he would live in residence or with students. I told him that that would probably be best.

Everything had come to a crushing standstill since I had opened Pandora's Box nearly two years ago. I desperately needed to get back to my art, my painting and my life. I told Joseph we had to move forward, and he agreed that it was time to move on.

My health continued to fail and I felt extremely ill. Every morning I awoke to a sick feeling in my stomach that continued all day. I had the unsettling feeling that all the 'Bill stuff' was not resolved. I took up walking again and continued reading psychology books. They seemed to bring a small measure of peace and comfort to my very troubled and tormented life.

Joseph and I saw a lot of each other. It was as if we were clinging to one other for survival through the abominable birthright situation that had taken hold of us. I took him for dinner again, and he told me that at the meeting with Bill's family, Bill's mother had taken him aside and told him that one night years ago, Bill had come home and told her that he had just had sex with me. His mother had asked him if he had used protection, and Bill had told his mother, 'No.' She had given Bill heck for it. I was shocked, not only because Bill's mother remembered something that had taken place twenty-four years ago, but also because she had revealed something so personal to Joey. Then the realization hit me. *They know. They know he's Bill's son.*

I told Joseph that Bill had a lot of growing up to do and not to expect too much. "I think Bill may have a very jealous girlfriend who cannot handle this, and that may be one of the reasons this is being held up."

Little did I know how very right I was.

An application form arrived in the mail from UBC, and Joseph filled it in. "Can you really afford to go out there?" I asked him skeptically. Joseph answered confidently:

"Mom, I could work in Richmond. Wouldn't it be neat if Bill and his wife shopped there? They would see me in the store." I was filled with immense sadness, hearing my son's words. *My son was hanging on to a dream—a fantasy. He was doing exactly what I had done for most of my life.*

We were both falling apart.

It was May 7, 1996. Joseph came by with his girlfriend Becki and told me he had received a phone call from Bill's girlfriend Laurie the night before.

"Mom, Laurie offered to fly me out there as a surprise for Bill's birthday," he announced unexpectedly.

Oh God, I was being cut out of the reunion! Why had I suspected this was going to happen? I was stunned and asked Joseph if this was a good surprise to pull on Bill, and he replied cockily:

"Hey, Bill's like me—calm—he can handle it." I was too dazed to speak. Becki noticed my anxiety and said sweetly:

"Joe, you can take a camcorder and record the reunion for your mother." I was deeply grateful that Becki spoke up for me. To my dismay, Joseph sneered sarcastically:

"I'm not going to do that."

I thought I was going to be sick and pleaded with him.

"Why not? If you don't want to use a camcorder, you can take a camera and have a photograph taken of the reunion for me." Again, he scoffed at the mere suggestion and steadfastly refused.

"No way! I'm not doing that for you."

I tried to sound happy for him and managed to weakly offer my congratulations. "It's not every day you get a father," I told him. In truth, I felt nauseated and sick to my stomach. I mentioned something about Ernest, and Joseph mockingly said that 'that was all old news.'

Later, after they left, I felt the horrendous pain. *I was being cheated out of introducing the two of them. Why? Hadn't I worked long and hard for two exhausting years to make it all come about?* I was in shock and convulsed in unutterable pain. It was my dream to introduce Joseph to his father, and Bill to his son, and this Laurie woman was taking all that away from me. And my own son had refused to record or take a picture of the reunion for me. Racked with grief, I wept all night until 4:30 a.m.

Two hours later I awoke, still crying. It was a big mistake, but I went to work that day, feeling very ill. In desperation, I spoke to the woman at the adoption agency again. She told me that Laurie was trying to control the situation and that this was the perfect way to do it. By inviting Joseph to Vancouver behind my back, Laurie could effectively leave me out of the reunion and control the course of events herself.

I had to speak to Joseph again. Surely, he would understand and not let them do this to me.

That same afternoon I telephoned Joseph and asked if he minded if I went to B.C. with him and stayed in a hotel nearby. His answer was annoyingly vague and distressing.

"I think I can manage it."

"Joseph, this is not Laurie's decision. She is not your mother, and she doesn't know you at all." To my bewilderment, he jeered at me:

"I'll think about it." *What was all that about—'I'll think about it'? And why was he mocking me?* Grudgingly, he agreed to give me a few days' notice so that I could book a plane fare.

What a God-awful nightmare everything had become, I thought morosely. Never in a million years would I have expected things to have turned out as they had. Bill's girlfriend obviously did not want me out there and this was her sneaky way of cutting me out of the reunion. Bill had told me to come out to B.C. with my son, and here was this woman taking all that away from me.

I was unable to push the tormenting thoughts out of my mind and desperately needed to leave work to go home and cry my heart out.

I sent Joseph's application form off to B.C. and silently wondered if the situation could possibly get any worse. It was already a horrifying, living nightmare.

There was an art meeting, and I decided to go to take my mind off things. Part way through the meeting, I was consumed with an ugly, sick feeling that something was amiss. I excused myself and called my son from the lobby of the museum.

"Joseph, I just want to see the two of you together for the first time. It would give me a sense of closure to the last two years of suffering." To my horror, he yelled at me:

"I don't want you at the introduction, and I don't want you out there! I'm a big boy now, and I can do this on my own. I need to do this for myself. This isn't about you—this is about me and Bill!"

Oh God, what was happening? Of course it was about me—it was my life! In desperation, I cried and begged him:

"Please, Joseph! Bill and I are your parents. I would be so pleased to see the two of you meet. I need to put an end to all of this—to see it finished." His voice was filled with a venomous rage as he shouted:

"Your job was finished when you did the DNA test! Why are you still hanging around? Stay out of it!" I was devastated by his heartless cruelty and abominable betrayal.

"Joseph, I'm not after Bill. What do you think I'm after?" I entreated.

"I don't know what you're after!" he barked.

"Please, Joseph! I would just introduce you and leave."

"You wouldn't leave! I don't want you out there. Leave it alone!" he ordered me.

"Joseph, why would you want Laurie, a total stranger, at the meeting and not me, your own mother who loves you?"

"I don't want her there either! This is about Bill and me!" I was reeling in shock and sick to my stomach. I got off the phone and staggered outside, knowing I was going to vomit.

I caught a cab home in a state of sheer panic. My son had betrayed me in the cruelest way imaginable, and I wanted to die. I was frantic and screamed to my friend Karen on the phone and told her if I had pills around, I would probably swallow them. She was terrified I was going to take my life and managed to talk me down. I nearly lost it that evening, having come so dangerously close to the edge. One slight nudge, and they would have pushed me right over.

I was extremely ill the following day and requested an emergency session with my therapist, Judi. She told me that Laurie was probably a decent woman and that I should just convey my dream to her—my dream of seeing the two of them together for the first time and being part of the introduction.

"Perhaps, Maureen, no one knows of your dream, and all you have to do is ask."

Ask? I was shocked. *I didn't realize I had the right to ask.*

"Maureen, you could either have Joey request that you be there for the introduction, or you could ask Laurie yourself."

"What if she says no, Judi?"

"Then you'll know she's a bitch, and you have every right to ask her why."

I told Judi how shockingly cruel Joseph had been to me the night before. Judi told me that although my emotions probably overwhelmed him, Joseph had no right to speak to me the way he had.

I got home and called Joseph and once again asked him if I could be there for the introduction. Thankfully, he had calmed down and agreed to ask Laurie on my behalf. Greatly relieved, I sat down and pondered over everything. I had been afraid my whole life and never felt that I had a right to ask for anything. In my family of origin, you never asked for anything, nor were you ever allowed to question.

Judi had taught me a very valuable lesson that day. I had the right to ask for what I wanted or needed, and I had the right to question when my want or need was denied. I never knew that before.

I decided to call Laurie myself.

11 *The Truth*

It was May 9, 1996. The phone call to Bill's girlfriend lasted an excruciating hour and a half.

Nervously, I dialed Laurie's number and she answered. I told her who I was, and to my relief, she sounded pleased. Casually, I made my request to be at the initial introduction of my son to Bill, his father, and her voice abruptly turned hostile.

"Yeah, I have a problem with that. I don't want you out here invading my space. This is about Bill and Joe, and it's my birthday surprise to Bill—a son. I really have a lot of problems of credibility with this immaculate conception bullshit. Any woman who had any knowledge of her anatomy would know whose child she was carrying."

Oh God, what was happening? Why was she so crudely shaming me? She had never set eyes on me. Her voice was bitter and filled with venom.

"You walked out on your new husband after three weeks and told him the ultimate lie. You cheated on him with Bill, and how do I know you're not coming out here to do the same thing to me? To walk into my house and do it again?" I was stunned by her vicious outburst and fought to remain calm.

"Laurie, I will stay at a hotel and just be there to support my son." To my shock, she shouted maliciously:

"I do not want you coming out here to stay in any hotel! I will be his support system. I am having a dinner party for eight, and you do not fit into my plan!" Again, I insisted that I would just be there to offer support for my son, and she adamantly refused. It was hopeless. There was incredible resentment and sarcasm in her voice as she admonished me severely.

"Did you ever stop to think what this would do to his family— sending a courier package like you did?" I was flabbergasted.

"Yes, Laurie, I spoke to my therapist, and morally and ethically, I was obligated to let Bill know he had a son. After the DNA test coming out as it did, how could I possibly tell my son there was no other father?"

"I want you to know that you are no threat to me," she lashed back. I was speechless as she continued to reprimand me, unabated.

"What was this story about child support?" she demanded to know. I was dazed.

"Child support? You mean the thing that happened this past year?"

Irately, she snarled, "I don't know. I only know little snippets here and there. It's obvious that you knew all along who the father was." *Oh God, I was under attack.*

"Laurie, I was only seventeen years old. I didn't know anything about my anatomy—I didn't know anything about sex. I think Bill, I told Bill, but, uh—" I stammered in painful confusion, and she interrupted in a harsh voice.

"He doesn't really remember. He's buying everything that you're saying." Valiantly, I tried to defend myself.

"He doesn't have to buy anything, Laurie. If Bill had any doubts, all he had to do was a DNA test, and I was willing to—" Impatiently, she cut me off.

"No, no, no! It's not that part of it. He was just buying the whole immaculate conception bullshit. He's buying into that 'cuz he's just like so thrilled to hear that '*Hey, maybe that could be my son.*'" Hurt and unnerved by her ruthlessness and undeserved hostility towards me, I patiently explained what had happened that night long ago. She laughed derisively.

"How could you not figure it out? I mean were there that many men at that time?" she demanded vehemently. I was flustered.

"That many what? There was no penetration, Laurie. Bill did not ejaculate. It was from penile lubrication. And I didn't even know what that was."

"But you must have known who the father was if he was the only one that you were like naked with, right?" I was growing more and more anxious with the intensely personal questions she was firing at me and her endless verbal assaults.

"No, no, no! What happened then is that three weeks later—okay now that happened, and like I said Bill tried and he was pushing to get in, and I didn't let him because I was a good, little Catholic girl and thought: *No, I can't let him do that.* But I didn't know that penile lubrication contained sperm. I never knew that. I had no idea. How, how would I know that at seventeen?"

"Okay," she conceded sarcastically.

"Okay. So somebody walked in on us. I don't know who it was. My back was to the door. Somebody walked in on us and that was it. It was over and we got up and we left. Bill had a girlfriend at the time—"

Infuriated, Laurie interrupted sharply. "Can I just interject one little thing here? Why did you leave with him when he had a girl-friend?"

She was shaming me again. "I was only seventeen—you do silly things—"

"I know! But at this point I'm saying he has a girlfriend right now, and here you are trying to get in again!" *Oh God, help me. What have I gotten myself into?*

"Oh! I'm not trying to get in again. I'm not trying to get in any—"

"That's how it feels to me!" she snapped irritably. Inexorably distressed at her malevolence towards me, I fought to continue.

"Laurie, let me go back. Bill had a girlfriend, Darlene—"

"Oh, I've met Darlene," she spat contemptuously.

"Yes, well, Bill had a girlfriend; I had a boyfriend. Well, let's put it this way—why did Bill do it? We're both at fault then, aren't we?

We're both at fault." She was furious with me for pointing out the discrepancy of culpability.

"I'm not in the game of attaching blame because I can't be bothered."

"Laurie, I was only seventeen, and I wasn't engaged or anything. I was just going out with Ernest—that's all. There was no permanent relationship." *Why was I justifying myself to this woman I had never met?*

She was combative and laughed scornfully at me because I hadn't figured all of this out when I was seventeen years old. When I mentioned to her that she would be Joseph's stepmother, she became extremely irate.

"No, not really. I mean he's an adult now. We're all adults now, and this is just a really nice thing for Bill to find, although his friends told him years ago—he knew about this young man."

What? What on earth was she saying?

"Bill knew? But—"

"He knew!" she bristled.

"Why wouldn't he ask? If—"

"His friends—because he thought you and Ernest were married, and he didn't want to go breaking that up. That's the story I got." I gasped in disbelief.

"Do you mean Bill actually had an inclination that this was his son?"

"Years and years ago—" She paused.

"I wish he would have said something," I said fervently.

"Well, he wished maybe you should have said something," she hissed.

"Well, I guess we both have regrets then." Shockingly, Laurie condoned Bill's shameful behaviour.

"But then again, don't forget—he's never been married, he's never had children and that was by choice. So, you know, it was one of those things where his friends—a few of his friends told him: *'Gee, Bill, that kid sure looks like you.'* And he really didn't feel like putting his head into that noose."

I was crushed. *Bill knew. Bill knew all those years he had a son, and he had done nothing to help me.*

To my dismay, the answering machine ran out of tape at that moment and started to beep. Laurie demanded to know what the sound was and if I was taping the conversation. I lied and explained that I was having problems with my machine. Appeased with my flimsy explanation, she continued talking. Still stupefied, I asked her:

"Exactly when did Bill realize that he had a son?"

"At least twenty years ago. His friends told him your kid looked just like him. That's when he said he never wanted children and never wanted to get involved. You have to realize that nothing was more important to Bill than his bank account." Amazingly, she continued to justify Bill's abhorrent behaviour.

"He was just a young man, and that's what these young men do." I was stunned that she could so easily condone Bill's inconceivably irresponsible, shameful behaviour. *What about me? I was only seventeen years old at the time.*

I explained my need for closure and the need to see the two of them together, and Laurie assured me I could have that closure when they all came out in July for a birthday party for one of Bill's brothers.

"You've suffered enough, Maureen. We're not going to give you any more grief. When we come out in July, I want to put my arm around you, walk you through the door and introduce you to Bill's family."

The harrowing conversation was finally over. I would never forget the pain or cruelty that this fanatically aggressive, jealous, vicious woman had inflicted on me. Laurie had stripped me of all dignity and had shamed me disgracefully. What happened between Bill and I occurred long before Laurie ever laid eyes on him, and it was none of her business. I would always be wary of this woman, and I would never trust her.

Laurie had, however, provided me with something invaluable—the truth. I realized why I had put up with her grueling abuse on the phone for an excruciating hour and a half. I was meant to know the truth—the truth about Bill. It was a restless sleep as I tossed and turned all night, muttering to myself: *Bill knew. He knew.*

Thankfully, Joseph was much calmer when he called the next morning. Laurie had left a message on his answering machine saying that she had spoken to me, and Joseph wanted to know what had happened. For a few seconds I debated telling him the truth, knowing that my silence would be a lie. I loved him too much to let him go out to Vancouver blind and told him of the conversation between Laurie and myself.

"Joseph, Laurie is a very powerfully aggressive and controlling woman." I repeated some of the nasty insults she had flung at me.

"But Mom, why would she be so nice to me?"

"Joseph, you'll figure it out, in time." He knew I was withholding something and pressed for an answer.

"Joseph, Laurie is only trying to get in good favour with Bill. And there are other issues." He continued to press. *Should I tell him?* I hesitated before reluctantly admitting:

"Joseph, Bill knew about you over twenty years ago. His friends told him that you looked exactly like him, and he told his friends that he never wanted children and wanted nothing to do with it." There was a long, uncomfortable silence.

"Oh well," Joseph said dejectedly. The euphoria was gone out of his voice. I got off the phone and wept for my son. I wept for me. I wept in agonizing despair from the pain Laurie had cruelly inflicted on me the previous evening. My sleep was extremely disturbed that night, and I was awakened by my own tormented screams.

Day after day, I dragged myself out of bed and went to work. In the evening, I walked to the park, read my psychology books and wept. Night after night, exhausted and drained, I tried in vain to sleep. I would crawl into bed, weeping, and would awaken, still weeping. Everything had become an unendurable, living nightmare and every morning I awoke in horror to discover that I was still stuck in the nightmare that would not end. I spent weekends in bed, too terrified to get up and face what lay ahead. I didn't know how to make the nightmare stop, and day and night became one.

And I dreamt of Bill.

A beautiful dream of a long-forgotten memory came to me. Little Joey was a baby, and we were at the zoo. I kept a watchful eye on him as he crawled in the grass next to me. Some of my friends sat on the plush lawn with me, and it was Darlene who had a camera and took a picture of little Joey. I noticed Bill and Cary standing about thirty feet away, looking on, and caught Bill intently observing the baby. I lowered my gaze and remembered thinking childishly to myself: *I wonder if Bill thinks this is his child.*

It was Mother's Day, and I wanted to do something special with Joseph before he left for B.C. for the reunion with his father. There had been so much arguing and fighting between us. I packed a picnic lunch and picked Joseph up after work. Together, we drove to Edworthy Park. Joseph built a fire, and we had a cozy, warm picnic of potato salad, smoked sausages and beans and sauntered down one of the trails for a peaceful walk in the woods. It was wonderful being with my son again. The sun was shining and the air was warm. This was all I wanted—to spend a few special moments with him without fighting before he left Calgary. We talked and I tried hard to speak well of Bill. Joseph said that he and Bill would 'cruise for girls' when he got to Vancouver and remarked flippantly:

"Mom, Bill said that I could be his son if I 'got a lot of girls.'" I thought to myself: *Great! All the values I taught him—gone out the window.* He became serious.

"Mom, if Bill isn't my father, you aren't my mother, and you may have taken the wrong child home from the hospital."

Oh God, what was he saying? I was upset and told him so. He had said this to me before, but I had never taken him seriously. He persisted.

"Mom, if your blood type is AB negative and I'm O, I can't be your son." *What a wonderful thing to say to your mother on Mother's Day, I thought wryly.* Alarmed at the implications of what he was saying, I felt sick to my stomach and refused to pursue it with him.

"Joseph, Laurie treated me very badly, and I tape recorded the conversation."

"That's your problem. She's been wonderful to me. That's

between you and her."

"Joseph, don't ever tell me how wonderful she is because I have proof to the contrary on tape. You should listen to the tape."

"No, I will never listen to it. Mom, if Bill had really known about me twenty years ago—so what. You gotta realize that 90% of guys would have done the same thing Bill did. Mom, if some guy mistakenly stepped in and claimed paternity and I knew I was the father, I would have done the same thing Bill did. I would have walked away and dumped the girl and the baby too." Appalled, I asked him:

"So you would abandon your child?"

"Sure. That's what Bill did. That's what I would do too."

I was dumbfounded but kept quiet. Joseph was over-identifying himself with Bill and therefore had to justify what Bill had done.

That night I had a dream. I was dressed in a long gown and Bill and I were dancing in perfect harmony. My dress swirled about his legs as he effortlessly guided me around. I knew I was not yet free of the past, and my dreams of Bill continued.

I was deeply troubled by my son's suggestion that I might not be his biological mother and the next morning I anxiously called the Calgary General Hospital where my son had been born. They informed me that I could get Joseph's blood type and birth records in a week or so by asking my doctor. Sick of my son's argument that I might not be his mother, I angrily phoned Joseph and told him I wasn't stupid and that I would prove him wrong in a few days. He was furious and hung up on me. I phoned him back and shouted at him:

"How dare you tell me that you would abandon your own child after your mother struggled all those years to raise you on her own! How dare you tell that to me! At least Ernest had the courage to sign a paternity agreement and change a few diapers. Bill is a coward—nothing but a God-damned coward!"

I knew it wasn't nice, but I had run out of patience. I could not allow Joseph to mistakenly think I agreed with the deplorable stand he had taken the day before. Joseph phoned back and tried to argue the blood type thing again. Exasperated, I raised my voice to him:

"I've had enough of this shit! I'm finished! I want nothing more to do with it!" and hung up on him.

I sat there, dazed at my outburst. I had always had great difficulty standing up to Joseph before that moment. Still and pensive for several minutes, I tried to figure out what had just happened. Then it came to me. For years I had carried enormous guilt that Joseph hadn't had a father, and I had always felt responsible. With Laurie's recent admission of Bill's truth, I realized that it was never my fault that Joseph hadn't had a father, but rather, both Ernest and Bill had, of their own free wills, abandoned their son. There was nothing for me to feel guilty about.

My son had been able to play the game with me all those years because I carried that guilt. Joseph had instinctively known that and had used it against me. I would no longer carry that guilt, nor would I allow anyone to blame or shame me again. I was through with dysfunctional behaviour, and I would not tolerate it again from anyone.

Joseph called again that evening with some startling news. "Mom, I got my blood typed and I'm an 'A'." *All those years, I thought he was an 'O'.* Cautiously, I asked him:

"What does that mean?"

"You don't have to worry, Mom—I'm your son."

"That's too bad," I replied ruefully.

"What do you mean?" He was stunned.

"Right about now, I'm wishing you weren't. Joseph, that was a rotten thing to do to me on Mother's Day. I have lost a lot of respect for you for saying that you would do the same thing Bill did and abandon your own child." Obstinately, Joseph argued:

"Mom, Bill thought Ernest and you were married and that's why Bill didn't step in." *Why did that sound so familiar? Weren't those Laurie's exact words to me?*

"Joseph, Ernest and I were together off and on for less than three years, and Bill saw me when you were about five years old. It was obvious he knew Ernest and I were not together. If anything goes wrong out there, make sure you have an extra $100.00 to change your return plane ticket." Furious, he yelled:

"I can see that I'm not going to get your support!"

I retorted, "Like you gave me?" I reminded him that when I told him Laurie had treated me badly, he had replied that *'that was my problem.'*

"Joseph, you took a complete stranger's side over your own mother's." He denied doing anything of the sort.

"Joseph, I want nothing more to do with any of this!" Angrily, I hung up on him.

A few minutes later I called him back and played the tape where Laurie admitted Bill knew all along he had a son but wanted nothing to do with it. I wasn't sure if Joseph heard or not. He had hung up. Relentlessly, I called him back and shouted:

"Laurie wasn't there! You weren't there! Only Bill and I were there!" and hung up on him once again. I was fed up. *How dare he tell me what happened before he was ever born. And it would be years before Laurie ever met up with Bill.*

That night, incredibly stressed, I walked for hours along the quiet, tree-lined neighbourhood streets where I lived. I gazed at the shimmering stars and the beautifully bright, perfectly spherical moon and struggled to find answers. Nothing came to me. Staring at the night sky, I felt numb and empty and wondered if God had abandoned and forgotten me.

None of them had wanted me involved in the reunion and I had been discarded. Fine. Joseph would have to handle his emotions himself. In the past, any overpowering emotion had always been vented as anger and fury towards me. Although I felt immense fear and apprehension at what was about to happen, I knew it was inevitable. It was in the hands of the gods now. My son was twenty-three years old and capable of handling his own emotions. I could no longer carry his pain for him.

The following day I realized that I had to confront Bill again. I went downstairs to the client phone room and tried desperately to calm my racing heartbeat. Feeling overwhelming anxiety, I picked up the phone and dialed Bill's number at work.

"Bill, is it true that you knew all those years you had a son but didn't step in because you didn't want that noose around your neck?"

The silence was deafening. Finally, Bill spoke in a soothing, gentle voice.

"No, Maureen, I had an inkling of the heart, that's all. And I couldn't act on an inkling." He was hesitant. "Who told you this?" he asked guardedly.

"Your girlfriend Laurie told me that you had known all those years. She said that it was your choice not to get married or have children and that you were too young and didn't want the responsibility."

"When did you speak to Laurie?" he asked suspiciously.

"I spoke to her privately about a week ago. Bill, I was young—only seventeen—and I accepted the responsibility, and it distressed and saddened me deeply to hear that you knew all those years you had a son." Bill was immediately defensive.

"How would I know that? I never saw him."

I corrected him, "Yes, Bill, you did see him, but you probably don't remember." Abruptly, his voice softened as he attempted to appease me.

"No, Maureen, it was only an inkling of the heart, and I couldn't walk in on your marriage with Ernest with just an inkling and destroy your marriage."

"That's too bad, Bill. I was being beaten and abused."

"I didn't know that!" he said, surprised.

"No, of course you wouldn't. I simply mean that you would not have interrupted anything. I never married Ernest. He was not the kind of man I ever would have married." Momentarily, I paused. "Bill, Laurie treated me with immense cruelty on the phone, and she demanded to know how many men I had been with. She felt that I was coming out there to get you."

Bill chuckled and answered arrogantly, "I guess she's just protecting her interests."

"Bill, I'm not after her interests," I said gravely. "I only want to know if you had known all those years because I had struggled so hard without any child support, and it hurt me to hear Laurie say you had known all along you had a son. She said your friends told you Joseph looked just like you and that you had not wanted to get involved." I hesitated. "Don't worry, Bill—I'm not coming after you for money." There was another long, deafening pause. Bill tenderly repeated his sweet words.

"No, Maureen, it was only an inkling of the heart. If I had known all those years, I would have helped you out." Without shame, he spoke disparagingly.

"Maureen, anyone could have had my kid." I was astounded and embarrassed at Bill's audacity to utter such belittling and reprehensible words to me, the mother of his only son. *I wasn't anyone.*

"So when's Joseph coming out, Maureen? I thought he was supposed to come out here. He had mentioned UBC?"

"Bill, that's between you and Joseph, and I don't want to interfere with that." He persisted.

"But when's he coming out?" I tried to sound disinterested.

"I don't know. But I'm sure that whenever he does come out, everything will work out fine." At that point, I quickly said good-bye. Bill's persistent questioning had unnerved me. I knew Joseph was leaving for Vancouver the following day, but I also knew if I revealed the surprise secretly arranged between Laurie and my son, there would be more hell to pay. And I just couldn't afford to pay any more hell than I already had.

The next day I instinctively knew something was not right. Bill had been too sweet to me on the phone. Perhaps I raised an alarm when I mentioned money to him. In any event, I knew Bill knew more than he was willing to admit.

It was May 22, 1996. Joseph was leaving that evening to meet Bill for the first time. I phoned my son for the last time and told him to have a good time and to call if he needed me. He said he would be fine and that he wanted to stop fighting with me. I told him that we fought because he didn't respect my feelings.

"Mom, I don't have any feelings, so why should I respect yours?" I was startled by his admission.

"Joseph, that's why we fight—you have to have respect for my feelings." He sounded disgruntled and only wanted validation about the blood type thing and wanted me to admit I was wrong. I countered that it was a rotten thing to do to me on Mother's Day—telling me that I might not be his mother. We spoke for a while and I got off the phone.

Part of me felt scared and nervous. I didn't know if I was scared for my son or if I was scared for me. I felt as if I were losing him, even though in my heart I knew I wasn't. I just wanted to hold him. All of this had been so very difficult. My dream for him was finally happening, and all I wanted to do was cry my heart out.

It was time for Joseph to leave for the airport for the reunion in Vancouver—the reunion that I would not be a part of.

It was finally time for Joseph to meet Bill.

12   *The Reunion*

I came home from work—numb, empty, exhausted. I tried to swallow a few bites of a sandwich and choked on the bread. Wearily, I turned on the T.V. and began watching the airline schedule channel. Flight arrivals, flight departures, estimated arrivals, estimated departures. I was able to determine when Joseph's flight would arrive in Vancouver and attempted to envision the reunion scene. Nothing came to me. Nothing at all.

Finally, weary of watching the airline schedules and knowing Joseph would have arrived safely in Vancouver, I went to bed, drained of all feeling.

A few hours later I awoke, crying. My grief was profound and continued throughout the night. Laurie had cruelly cheated me out of a very beautiful, precious moment—a moment that could never be relived. I would never know. That moment was lost forever. I had fervently hoped that Joseph would call, but he didn't. It was an insufferable evening of agonizing despair as I wept for hours on end.

Miraculously, I survived the horrendous night and managed to stop the flow of tears before going to work the following day. If there was a lesson to be learned from the brutal suffering, the lesson escaped me.

I had to start living for me. For so many years, I had lived for my son and had concentrated so much of my life being a loving, nurturing mother to him. In the end, all I got was a good, hard kick in the teeth. Perhaps I had not concentrated enough on me. Perhaps I had loved him too much, if there was such a thing.

I managed to make it through the day at work and went home, exhausted. It would take a very long time to heal from what had happened. It had been a long and torturous journey during which I had grown enormously, and my spirit needed time to rest and time to heal.

In the midst of my thinking, Joseph called. The last thing I wanted to hear was his voice. He asked me how I was and I answered coolly, "Fine."

"How are you holding up, Mom? Are you sure you're okay?" Not happy to hear his cheerful voice, I answered miserably:

"Please don't say anything about Laurie. I don't want to hear it." Joseph turned hostile.

"I don't need to hear this out here!" he bellowed. There was an uncomfortable silence, and I attempted to keep the conversation going and asked him innocently:

"Did you have a talk with your father?"

Angrily, Joseph shot back, "About what?"

I realized that he presumed I meant—had he addressed the abandonment issue with Bill? I was caught off-guard by his angry response and casually asked him if he looked like his dad, and he answered, "Yes." He was quiet again, and there was yet another uncomfortable silence. I decided to confront him.

"You have been very cruel to me through this, Joseph. You have treated me very badly for a very long time. You have taken all your anger out on me for many years because you did not have a father. Well, now you got what you wanted. I carried a lot of unearned guilt all these years because you didn't have a father, and it wasn't my fault. I'm letting go of that guilt, and I'm not taking your crap anymore." Joseph was outraged.

"I don't want to hear that garbage out here!" he yelled. Undeterred, I answered in a detached voice, "Fine. Good-bye," and hung up on him.

Less than five minutes later, Laurie called, and in a too-sweet, slurpy voice, she cooed:

"Hi Maureen. This is Laurie calling from Vancouver. I just wanted to let you know that you have the most wonderful son. He is just incredible. I don't know if he called you today—I told him to—I think they're going out tonight—"

I was alarmed to hear her voice and frantically tried to hang up the phone. *Oh no! The hideous voice wouldn't stop—she was speaking through the answering machine!* In desperation, I yanked the cord from the wall and the machine went dead.

It was 12:20 a.m. and I lay on the couch, feeling totally decimated. In hopeless despair, I wept broken heartedly all night.

I awoke the next morning, sick as a dog. Having had only three hours of sleep since Joseph left, I gagged while trying to sip a few mouthfuls of juice and never felt so ill in my entire life. I managed to get dressed and drove to Edworthy Park. It was 9:30 a.m., and it was a bright, beautiful, sunny day. As I wandered aimlessly along the path through the tall, wild grasses, I cried in heartbreaking anguish: *God, please tell me why the suffering has not yet ended!* Then I heard it. The faint, unmistakable sound in the not too far-off distance.

It was the train coming. I glanced over the field of wild grasses and hesitated. I could easily walk the seventy-five feet or so and get to the tracks on time. At the last second, I could walk in front of the train, and it would all be over. The pain would be gone. So they'd have to scrape me off the tracks, and the conductor would probably not have a good life after he killed me, but so what. My suffering would be over. I sank to my knees in excruciating pain. *Please God, take away my unbearable suffering!* I stumbled to the end of the path and slumped wearily onto the bench near the river and lay down. The sun shone warmly upon my face. I was dazed and confused and lay there for several hours, unable to move. I was too numb and exhausted to feel anything that night.

For the next two days I wandered aimlessly about the pathways in the park. Each time I crossed the train tracks, I hesitated and waited for the train. It never came. Drained of all energy, I stood motionless in the stillness and listened to the birds and crickets in the pond a short distance down the path. The trees were budding and the first leaves had sprung. On one of those days, I took a different path home and came to a crossroads where the path branched off in three directions. At one side were two benches. A woman sat on one of the benches.

I decided to sit down and speak to her. She saw the sadness in my face and questioned me. Tearfully, I told her my story. Her words were filled with a gentle understanding.

"Maureen, I feel your pain. You have come to the crossroads of your life. You can choose this path, or you can choose that path. You have to tell your son, *'I need a long rest, and I have to nurture me now. You have your life, and I wish you well in it. I have to take care of me now.'*"

I told her how I had expected a thank-you call from Bill, and she said, "Maureen—think! You cannot expect people to treat you as you would treat them. These are cruel, selfish people, and you want nothing to do with them. Laurie's call was to rub your nose in it, and it was cruel. It would be good for your son to move out there and live with his father—he will finally grow up and learn some hard lessons."

She continued talking and I was immensely grateful for her kind words. "All your suffering will make you stronger, Maureen. You are a beautiful, young woman, inside and out." It was so nice to hear someone say that to me, even if it was a stranger. Sadly, I told her that I didn't feel that way.

"Maureen, you and your son are so entrenched with each other, it is time to let him go. Stop doing things for him, and start doing things for you." I thanked her and she hugged me tightly. I cried and told her she was a blessing from God.

She corrected me, "Maureen, you are a blessing from God." I got home and felt that things were going to be okay. I believe God put that woman on that path that day for me.

For the first time in a very long time, I slept a few, fitful hours of sleep.

I found out that Joseph had been home for two days and had not bothered to give me a call.

Finally, he rang. I held him accountable for the pain he had caused me. He began shouting, accused me of pushing him further away and insisted that he had done nothing wrong. It was hopeless. Several days elapsed, and neither of us spoke to the other.

The thought that my son would soon be leaving for B.C. while we were not speaking filled me with unspeakable grief. Finally, I got ahold of him. Unhappily, I told him I felt I was losing him to Bill and that I didn't want him going out to B.C. without us first talking. His voice was condescending.

"That was your doing, Mom. You told me you needed to work on some stuff."

I implored him, "I haven't seen you since Mother's Day."

Scornfully, he rebuked me, "That was your choice."

He was making me beg.

"Joseph, everyone got closure out of this except me. You got your father, Bill got his son and I got kicked out of it. That really hurt. The night you left, I sat watching the arrivals and departures on T.V. for two hours and cried all night and the next night as well. All I wanted was to see the two of you together for the first time. That moment is gone and can never be relived—and it will always hurt." Joseph changed the subject abruptly.

"Mom, they're coming out here in July, and you can see me and Bill together then."

Sadly, I told him, "Joseph, Laurie won't allow that to happen. She doesn't want Bill to see me."

"Mom, that's not her decision. There's no reason why you can't see us together. I'll introduce you to Bill."

What was he saying? I already knew Bill.

Apparently, the visit with Bill went well. When Joseph told me that Bill had hugged him when he first met him, my voice broke with unspeakable sadness.

"Joseph, that's the moment I missed—the moment I wanted to see." Joseph was silent. I realized he couldn't deal with my emotions when he changed the subject yet again.

"Mom, Bill's left-handed. I told Bill you had encouraged me to be right-handed as a child, and Bill wondered why you had done that."

"Joseph, perhaps that's why your writing was so bad—you were supposed to be left-handed. Left-handed people use a different part of their brain. Well, now we know." There was another long pause.

"Mom, Laurie's jealous." I was startled by my son's admission.

"Joseph, I already knew that. She treated me with terrible cruelty." He persisted.

"Mom, she wanted to have Bill's child, and they had agreed not to have children."

"Joseph, Laurie's jealousy does not excuse her cruelty. Jealousy only ruins things."

Joseph told me he was moving out there soon. I knew it would be really hard on me and I told him so. "You'll handle it Mom," he said reassuringly.

"I'm not so sure," I replied dismally.

I got off the phone and went outside. It was dark and I curled up on the lawn chair under the stars, snuggled under a warm blanket. I lay there for several hours. I was happy all went well with Bill, and it felt good to hear the two of them got along. I thought about my son leaving, and I cried myself to sleep.

The following day I arrived at work and decided I needed to speak to Bill. Using the client phone for privacy, I dialed his number and he answered.

"Bill, how did you like our boy?" I asked playfully. Bill chuckled.

"Joe's a real nice kid. We got along just fine."

"I guess you two have a lot in common." I detected a slight aggravation in Bill's voice as he answered curtly:

"Somewhat."

Puzzled by Bill's cool response, I asked, "I guess you two look alike?"

"A little." I requested a private meeting with him and Joseph when he came out in July, and Bill agreed that we needed to meet privately. "Laurie and I have already discussed it and feel it is necessary— a meeting with you, Joe and myself."

"Bill, that was the reason I called Laurie several weeks ago—to ask her if I could be there for the initial meeting to introduce the two of you. That's all I wanted, Bill, and she said, 'No.'"

Again, Bill reassured me. "Maureen, we'll have a private meeting and we'll have lunch together." I was overjoyed and voiced my sentiment.

"Bill, you're filling a hole in Joseph's soul that has been there a long time."

"That's good," Bill answered quietly.

"This should be good for you too," I told Bill, my voice quivering with emotion. "I know this has been very hard on everyone and it came out of left field." Bill quickly changed the subject.

"Was Joe accepted at UBC?"

"I don't know yet—it will be awhile. I wish you both luck in the future, Bill," I said heartily and hung up.

Throughout the conversation, Bill's annoyance and reservation were a far cry from the sweet, gentle Bill who had spoken to me several weeks earlier. I couldn't be bothered to ask Bill what was wrong. I only wanted that meeting, and I felt so much better having asked for it. I was beginning to feel confident asking for what I wanted or needed. After all, I was Joseph's mother, and they couldn't pretend I did not exist.

Little did I know how terribly wrong I was.

Later that day I had another emergency session with my therapist. Judi told me that if Bill was going to have a relationship with Joseph, he would have to deal with me as well, as Joseph's mother. I could not understand how Bill could treat his son with respect and had no respect for me—the mother of his only child. It made no sense. No sense at all. Judi had no answer for me.

I felt a small measure of peace that evening after having spoken to Bill earlier in the day and went to bed at 10 p.m. Dead tired from the lack of sleep, I collapsed into a nearly comatose slumber.

What on earth was that ghastly annoying sound? The stillness of the night was shattered by the jangling of the phone ringing off the hook. It rang and rang incessantly and refused to quit. Crudely awakened, I groggily got up, switched on the light and fumbled for the phone.

"Hi Maureen. This is Laurie from Vancouver—"

Oh God, no! It was that hideous voice again—it was Laurie! I cut her off immediately.

"I have nothing to say to you, ever again!" and angrily slammed the phone down on her ear. She called back and shouted:

"I don't care—" I stopped her dead in her tracks and again slammed the phone down. *What on earth was the woman doing? It was nearly midnight. Did she actually think I would talk to her after what she had done to me?* I went back to bed, satisfied and amazed with myself. I had my power and control back, and I would never relinquish it to her again. There must have been a squabble going on over there in the Lentz household. I thanked God for giving me the chance to snatch my power back from her and, smiling contentedly, fell into a deep sleep.

It was a beautiful, peaceful slumber.

There would be no more harassing calls that night, but Laurie would, in time, find a way to get even.

13   *Aftermath*

I had been experiencing severe anxiety attacks for months and plunged into a worsened state of panic and depression as the relationship with my son continued to deteriorate.

It had been several weeks since I had seen Joseph, and I missed him terribly. I called to invite him for a barbecue, and my invitation was met with indifference.

"I'll see if I have time for you." I felt slighted and wished I hadn't asked. Later that same evening, I again asked if he had time to see me. He was annoyed and abrupt with me.

"I'm watching a movie—I don't have time." Morosely, I realized I was begging for his time and that he was still punishing me, as he had done for years. My panic and anxiety increased as he withdrew further from me. It was as if he no longer needed a mother, now that he had found a father.

Needing acknowledgment of the pain Joseph had caused me, I tried to hold him accountable again and called him later that evening.

"Joseph, you and Laurie were extremely cruel to me." He angrily denied having done anything wrong.

"You didn't understand! I wanted this for me. What do you want?"

"Joseph, that night you were cruel to me, I wanted to die. Several times at Edworthy Park, I wandered onto the train tracks and contemplated ending it all." He laughed contemptibly.

"Mom, I sure hope you're still seeing your therapist."

Ruefully, I replied, "You're extremely selfish. You always have been." Joseph started shouting and I said simply, "Gotta go!" and hung up.

Later that day I spoke to my therapist. "It's no use telling Joey of your pain. He doesn't get it, and he doesn't have to get it. You do. Keep moving forward. Leave him be for now." I told Judi I had nothing more to give my son.

Fervently, she urged me, "So, Maureen, you give to you now." Judi was right. The relationship with my son had been severely co-dependent for years, and I could not live like that anymore. I could no longer tolerate Joseph's abuse, and I could no longer carry his pain for him. Carrying his pain was killing me.

I told Judi I planned on visiting my gallery in Vancouver and having a little vacation out there, as I had done for years. She felt it was a good idea and would help me heal. Anxiously, I told Judi of my anxiety attacks, and although concerned, she countered, "But you're getting through it." I was unable to share her view and wasn't convinced. But she was the psychologist.

That evening I walked to a beautiful park a short distance from my house and watched some young fellows play basketball. They reminded me of my son and I was overcome with despondency. I positioned myself under a huge oak tree and listened to the blustery wind whistling through the leaves and the moaning of branches swaying in the wind. Grief-stricken, I sat in the windswept grass and wept. I still needed to see Bill, but I wanted to face him alone, without Joseph there. The past had yet to be acknowledged and had yet to be resolved.

Suddenly, a strong gust of wind blew away my jacket, and I scrambled after it. The sky overhead darkened, and the charcoal-gray clouds looked heavy and ominously like rain. The wind picked up, the young fellows left, and alone in the vast expanse of field, I wearily got up and retreated to the only warm, safe place I knew—home.

Since Joseph steadfastly refused to see me, I decided to surprise him at work the following day. We went for a supper break to the Pig & Whistle Pub next door, and he started yapping about Bill and

Vancouver. At one point in the conversation, Joseph mentioned having his graduation ceremonies at UBC.

"Are you going to behave out there, Mom?" he asked me.

"That's very disrespectful, Joseph. Will my family be there?" I knew he was referring to his first convocation ceremonies where I had refused to acknowledge his grandmother and aunts. I let his remark go and told him I was taking a vacation to Vancouver to visit my gallery.

"Are you going to see Bill?" he asked suspiciously.

"What for?" I shot back. Joseph was silent. It was obvious he was jealous and perceived me as invading his territory when it came to Bill. It was evident he did not want me to see his father.

Joseph continued talking about Bill, and after listening for a while, I became strangely silent. I felt sick to my stomach and couldn't eat. Joseph stared quizzically at me and asked what was wrong. "Nothing," I answered sadly, shaking my head and fighting back tears.

"Did I say something?" he asked, to which I replied miserably, "No."

"Mom, are you unhappy I had a good time out there?"

"No, I'm happy you had a good time." I started to cry and we hastily left the restaurant. Outside, standing in the warm sunshine, Joseph was silent, and for the first time that I could remember, he didn't make fun of my feelings. I got into my car and drove home, tears streaming down my face.

The following day I found out Joseph had been in a motorcycle accident and I rushed over to his house. His arms were badly scraped and bloodied, and he owed his friend for the repair of the motor bike. I drove him to work to try to cheer him up. He was somber and quiet, and I decided it was a good time to speak my mind.

"Joseph, the honour of introducing you to your father belonged to your mother over your father's girlfriend. In the future, I expect that any similar honour will rightfully be paid to me, as your mother and the one who raised you. I will never take second place to Laurie again."

Joseph was sullen and didn't speak.

The next morning I spoke to my therapist and was taken aback by her candor.

"Maureen, Bill wants nothing to do with you. He has a relationship with this woman, and in order to maintain it, he will stay well away from you." Her words stung sharply and I cried in alarm:

"What about occasions that arise—wedding, graduation and the like? He can't exclude me from those things!" Judi's answer was forthright.

"No, he can't. You will be involved where it concerns your son, but where it concerns her, you will not be involved." I told Judi that I had expected a phone call at the very least, and she was conciliatory. "Of course you did. A phone call would have been in order. But don't expect it." Feeling a tremendous dejection, I lamented:

"I gave up twenty years of child support, and I could have been selfish and gone after the money. Instead, I did the unselfish thing to give Bill and Joey some happiness. Judi, it's wrong for Bill to treat Joey with respect and me like shit!" Judi agreed wholeheartedly but was at a loss to explain Bill's behaviour.

"Maureen, we'll have to work on you in therapy to get some resolution to this because the meeting may never take place at the end of July. Bill may cancel, and if he does, you should call him and hold him accountable. Ask him why you had not gotten together as promised." I told Judi I couldn't count on Bill coming through and that in the past year everything he had told me had been a lie.

I continued to feel severely ill for the next several days and finally made my decision. In desperation, I called Judi again.

"Judi, I can't handle this anymore. I don't eat, I don't sleep, there has been no resolution for me and I feel sick all the time. I'm going to see Bill while I'm in Vancouver."

"Go for it! You know better than anyone what you need. You need this. Do it for you. Phone him and ask him for an appointment for lunch."

"No! I want to surprise him. If I phone first, he could make an excuse or run." Judi questioned the surprise but encouraged me to do what I needed to do.

Two more days elapsed. I woke up feeling a frightening and

horrible stress, worse than anything I had ever experienced. I was anxiously looking through baby pictures and couldn't find the one of me carrying Joey in my arms when he was about eight months old. I began to panic and weep uncontrollably and frantically tore the house apart, searching for the missing photograph. For several hours I hunted in vain.

I rushed to the car and drove in a frenzy to Joseph's house. Joseph's roommate Brian allowed me to search in Joseph's room, but I found nothing.

I proceeded downstairs and the bright, familiar colours of a development envelope on the stereo unit caught my eye. I opened it, not expecting to find anything. To my shock, there were two pictures of Bill amongst the roll of developed pictures. I gasped and, in one swift, deft movement, slipped them into my purse.

Just then, Brian stepped into the room. Furtively, I put the envelope down, saying, "No, these aren't them." Thankfully, Brian didn't see me take the photographs. Safely back in the car, I drove in a flurry to duplicate the pictures of Bill. I felt an overwhelming sense of relief. *Now I knew what Bill looked like. No one could take that from me.* Unable to take my eyes off the pictures, I stared at them in awe and disbelief. *So this was what my son's father looked like. This was the other half of my son's identity that I never fully understood.*

Later that evening I found the old photograph of Joey in my arms that I had been frantically searching for. It had been carefully tucked away in a small, white photo album. Scrupulously, I spent the next several hours examining all my old photographs and extracted those most precious to me and painstakingly arranged them all together in the little album. I perched the photo album in clear view on the bookcase where I could easily see it.

Just as I began to calm down, Joseph called and yelled that he knew I had taken his photographs and that he wanted them back.

"You can come by and pick them up—they'll be in the mailbox," I assured him. He relented somewhat and finally agreed that I could keep one of the photographs. Sometime during the night, he came by and retrieved it. Meanwhile, I hid in my house with the lights turned low to avoid seeing him.

The following day I spoke to a friend who advised me not to surprise Bill when I visited Vancouver and to instead phone him and ask for a change of plans. I decided my friend was right, and summoning all the courage I could, I picked up the phone to call him.

"Bill? It's Maureen."

"Hi, how are you." His voice was dead-sounding. I ignored it.

"Fine. Bill, I just have a request of you. Do you have a minute?"

He was resentful and snarled bitterly, "No, not really!"

I was taken aback by his anger but nonetheless continued:

"Bill, I won't take long. I'm going to be in Vancouver on Friday and I wonder if you and your wife *[girlfriend, really]* would have the generosity of spirit to give me an hour of your time. I would just like to feel at peace with this and give you some pictures of Joey and have a talk." Bill was furious.

"I don't know! I'll have to ask her and call you back!"

"Bill, I'm not demanding or threatening anything—just to have a talk—"

"I don't know! I'll have to call you back! What's your number?" I told him. He fumed, "I'll call you back!"

The evening wore on and there was no phone call. The words of a beautiful, comforting quote came to me: *Be not deceived; God is not mocked; for whatsoever a man soweth, that shall he also reap.*[3]

It was the day before my vacation. Extremely despondent, I put in a frantic call to Judi.

"Maureen, the reason you're so confused and having such a hard time of this mess is because you have to learn to say 'good-bye' to Bill, and you didn't get to say 'hello.'" I burst into tears. Judi continued thoughtfully:

"Leave him be. You've turned his life upside down. Perhaps in the future things will change—but for now, best to leave him be. You're much further along than he is. This will take time."

It was Friday, June 28, 1996 and the start of a month's vacation. I left for Vancouver on the early morning flight and was incredibly nervous upon my arrival. Immediately, I caught a cab to my Bed and Breakfast in Kitsilano. It was a lovely, little suite, tastefully and elegantly decorated, with a huge king-size bed. After unpacking a few things, I left for Granville Island to visit my gallery and desperately tried to push thoughts of seeing Bill out of my mind. As the day wore on, I became more and more confused and anxious. I went into Opus, a well-known art store tucked amid an assortment of shops on the Island, and purchased over $100 in art supplies. I walked back outside, sat on a bench and began to cry. I couldn't afford the purchase and had no idea why I had spent all the money that was meant for my vacation on art supplies. Embarrassed and ashamed, I wiped my tear-stained face and brought all the paints back inside the store for a refund. Without a word, the girl behind the counter refunded my money.

I headed back to the B&B and dropped off the only purchase I had kept—a few sheets of art paper. Then I started out on a long walk and found myself headed downtown. *God, no, I was going to do it— I couldn't help myself!* I caught a cab and asked the driver to take me to the Sandman Inn, next door to where Bill worked. Nervously, I hurried past his building to check the address and retreated back to the Inn. It was nearly 4 p.m. Too terrified to wait in the lobby of his building, I stood inconspicuously at the bus stop across the street from the hotel. Finally, at 4:15 p.m., I went back across the street to the lobby of Bill's building and waited patiently until 5 p.m. Finally, the security guard took me up to Bill's office. To my shock and dismay, the girl said he had left at 4 p.m. I stared at her in disbelief. *No, that's not possible! How could I have missed him? There must have been a back door to the building I had foolishly overlooked.* Crushed and heartbroken, I didn't bother leaving my name and left.

Wearily, I walked back to the B&B by way of the Burrard bridge, a distance of several miles. It was a burning, hot day, and I paused for a short rest on the immense bridge. I peered over the railing and wondered what it would be like plunging several hundred feet to the water below. Surely, one would not survive such an incredible fall. Nervously, I hastened from the bridge and continued the long, exhausting trek home. Fatigued and filled with unspeakable grief, I cried myself to sleep. Hours later, I was surprised to be awakened by my hostess, knocking at the door. She had a phone call for me. It was my son, Joseph.

"Mom, don't go to see Bill," he urged me fervently. *I didn't tell him I had already tried and failed miserably.*

"Joseph, I just wanted resolution—to see Bill one more time."

"Mom, please don't go to see him. You'll make a fool of yourself if you do. I can possibly arrange a meeting for you." *Why was he being so adamant? I wondered. Why did it matter so much to him?*

"No, Joseph, it's up to Bill—not you." Joseph could tell I was in a terrible emotional state and implored me again not to see Bill—that it would not be a good idea and that he would see to it that I got a meeting with Bill. Slightly heartened by my son's promises, I got off the phone and went back to bed. *Bill was right here in Vancouver and I couldn't see him until Tuesday because Monday was a holiday and I had no idea where Bill lived.* I felt a measure of comfort having heard my son's consoling voice. Never would I have expected him to call me here. Although I never suspected anything at the time, it would become shockingly clear to me later on that Joseph had an ulterior motive for discouraging a visit with Bill.

The following day was Saturday and I needed to get out of Vancouver, so I took the ferry to Victoria. I tried to hide my tears from other passengers on the ferry and was consumed with thoughts of Bill. I walked the length of the ferry and back, nervously searching for him. I sensed my behaviour was irrational, but part of me couldn't help thinking that he would be just around the next corner. Finally, I realized how ridiculous I was being and gave up and forced myself to sit down on a bench on the outside deck. Watching the sea's rhythmic, undulating waves, I felt mesmerized and frozen in time. The forces of nature were wondrous, powerful and beautiful and gave me a small measure of hope. *Surely, there were mightier things out there in the Universe, far more powerful than I, to help guide me and keep me safe through this terrifying and torturous journey to hell.*

Once in Victoria, I visited some of my favorite places, including the spectacular, fragrantly-scented rose garden next to the Empress

Hotel and Barb's Place for fresh halibut. It was an okay day, and exhausted, I took the ferry back to Vancouver.

The next day was Sunday, and I decided to walk along Kitsilano Beach, two blocks from my B&B. For miles I walked, stopping to talk to people along the way. I wanted to see Wreck Beach on the farthermost edge of the point. I spoke to a kind woman named Linda on Point Grey Road, and she invited me in for tea and a talk. She was a lovely, compassionate woman and urged me to get back to my life and put everything behind me.

I continued on my journey and met a fellow named Rob, who guided me to Wreck Beach. It was a beautiful, sunny day, and I felt alive for the first time in a very long time. I was determined to reach the beach, and after climbing over and under tree roots, driftwood and rocks and rounding numerous points, the beach finally came into view. It was like walking back in time and was truly magnificent. There was a strange array of wooden poles sticking out from the sand that, from a distance, resembled giant toothpicks. The afternoon sun glinted off the rippling waves that gently lapped the shore. There was water as far as the eye could see, stretching to eternity. I stood there in awe, standing on the edge of the world. My long day's journey had finally come to a glorious end.

Numerous hippie-like people sauntered about the beach, some smoking pot and others drinking and laying about nude. I felt an incredibly strange sensation that I had been transported back in time to my youth, yet in a different form. This was something I had long left behind me, and I had the wonderful opportunity of viewing it all over again from a different perspective.

Rob and I found a secluded, little patch of sandy beach and talked. The water began rising, and not wanting to be caught by the incoming tide, we climbed up the rocks to the top of the cliff. As we roamed through the University grounds, I had a good look at the school my son would be attending. I felt some peace, knowing this was where he would be. Rob and I had coffee and parted company, and I took the bus back to Kitsilano Beach. I decided to leave for home the following morning because I knew the temptation would be far too great to see Bill on Tuesday at work.

The next day I left for home and shamefully hid my tears from the stewardesses on the plane. *There would be no resolution or closure for me on this trip, I thought morosely.* I felt overwhelmingly fatigued, depressed and so very much alone.

When I arrived home, I phoned Joseph and asked him if he had talked to Bill, and he said, "No." After repeated questioning, he finally admitted that he and Laurie had been e-mailing each other. I admonished him for his secrecy.

"Mom, you asked me if I had talked to them. And I had only e-mailed them—that's not talking." I told Joseph his distortion of the truth was still a lie and begged him to keep me informed as to what was going on. He grudgingly agreed, but I wasn't sure I could trust him or believe him. He had told so many lies throughout the whole reunification, it was obvious that he wanted me to have no part in it. I realized that that was why he had discouraged a visit with Bill while I was in Vancouver. He wanted it all for himself. Everything was always for him. Joseph would stop at nothing to ensure he was always the center of attention. He would let nothing and no one get in his way.

Two days later Joseph asked if he could live with me at the end of the month in order to save money for B.C. Caught off-guard by his request, I hesitated. "Joseph, we'll have to talk about it."

He retorted, "Then I'll just have to move out to B.C. sooner." *There it was—the old manipulation.* This time, I didn't fall for it and answered, unperturbed:

"Maybe that's what you need to do—get out to B.C."

"No, no! I'd rather stay here and get lots of hours and make some money." I told him it wasn't a good idea—that I was still healing. He wasn't happy, but I knew it wasn't a good idea for us to live together for any length of time under the circumstances.

Plagued with an excruciating despondency all weekend, I called Joseph on Monday and asked him how his week was. He was curt and abrupt with me and told me he was busy all week. I asked him what he was doing on Wednesday evening, and he told me he was picking Bill up at the airport at 8:30 p.m. I felt a deep sadness and wondered if Bill would call me for a meeting as he had promised.

Wednesday finally arrived. I woke up feeling very sick and cleaned all day to try to take my mind off things. Finally, I called Joseph at 10:45 p.m. His roommate told me he had gone out with his 'Dad' to Brewster's Pub. I thanked him and hung up.

The following morning Joseph called, wanting another favour. Apparently, he had left Becki's car downtown because he drank too much the previous evening and wanted a ride to get it.

"Weren't you with Bill?" I asked him.

"Yes, for a while, but my friends joined me, and Bill had to leave." Point-blank, I asked Joseph:

"Is Bill an alcoholic?"

Joseph was stunned and retorted sharply, "What makes you say that?"

I answered simply, "I believe he is an alcoholic." Joseph was furious.

"You don't even know him!" *And you do?* I felt slighted by his snide remark.

"I don't have to. He exhibits all the traits. There's a lot of things you and Bill could do besides drink." Amazingly, Joseph agreed.

"Are you going to see Bill tonight?" I asked him.

"I don't know—he's going to call." Discouraged with his aloofness and secrecy, I left him at Becki's car and drove home.

It was Saturday and I woke up, overwhelmingly distraught. Bill was leaving town the following day and I still hadn't heard anything. In panic and desperation, I decided to try and catch Joseph before he began work and ran into him in the parking lot outside the store. Anxiously, I asked him:

"Joseph, have you heard of any meeting? Has Bill said anything to you?"

He answered curtly, "Not that I know of."

"What did you do yesterday?" I asked him curiously. He hesitated, not wanting to reveal anything.

"We all went to Drumheller." I felt so left out hearing they all spent the day together and frantically beseeched him:

"Joseph, would you encourage a meeting with Bill?"

"No. I don't want to get involved." I felt a heartbreaking anguish as I watched him turn his back on me, in total indifference to my plight. I was devastated by my son's shocking betrayal and, reeling, staggered back to my car. Later I called him at work, and we had a stinking fight.

Horribly distressed, I drove to Bragg Creek and tried to calm myself. *Tomorrow it will all be over—Bill will be gone.* It gave me a small measure of comfort. Bill was a gutless, spineless coward, and I hated what he had done to me.

Finally, Sunday arrived. Bill never had any intention of seeing me or having a meeting with me. Everything had been a lie—a stinking, rotten lie.

I drove to 17th Avenue to find a frame shop and stood perplexed in front of some buildings, unable to find the art store. Suddenly, the whole world stopped and everything moved in a slow, grinding motion around me. Shockingly disoriented, I was filled with unspeakable terror and couldn't comprehend what was happening to me. I couldn't remember where I had left the car or why I was standing on the street. Anxiously, I inspected the numbers on the buildings and paced back and forth but was unable to determine if the numbers were going up or down. I held my head in my hands and tried to stop the thundering noise. *Was I losing it? Was I going mad?* It was the worst panic attack I had ever experienced. The terror finally subsided and I managed to find the store I was looking for, remembered where I had parked the car and frantically drove home while I still remembered where I lived.

It was Monday and one of the worst days of my life. Reality hit and hit hard. I was feeling the lowest I had ever felt and put in an emergency call to Judi. I told her I was better off dead and that I had been thinking all day about the best way to kill myself. Judi insisted I get in to see her right away. Fifteen minutes before I was about to leave for my appointment, Joseph called. I screamed at him:

"There's insurance on my credit line but no insurance on the house! I'm sorry I've been a bad mother! If anything happens to me, you have Bill!" I let out a terrible cry and threw down the phone. Deeply despondent, I left to meet up with Judi. She was furious with me.

"You've really done a number on yourself!" I hung my head in horrific shame while she angrily admonished me.

"Joseph called me, worried!" In a flat, deadened voice, I remarked:

"Wow. It's the first time he's ever shown me any concern." Judi continued to rebuke me.

"That was really hurtful—what you screamed at Joey!" I stared at her blankly and, in an empty, emotionless voice, replied:

"I really don't care." She tried a different approach.

"Maureen, I warned you that this might happen!" I wanted to leave her office. She was shaming me, and it wasn't helping, not one bit. Sadly, I told her:

"Judi, I was just too weak, after all the hurtful things that had been done to me, to handle the reality of the end of it." It was a lousy session and I wasn't happy with Judi. She did help me to compose a final closure letter to Bill—one which I would read to him over the phone when I got home. It read:

[Dated July 22, 1996]
Bill, this is Maureen
Bill, you have lied to me
You have acted cowardly
You have been very disrespectful of me
You have hurt me immensely
I have lost all respect for you, Bill
My son might recognize you as his father
I never will

On the copy to be mailed, I added, '*Let's hope our paths never have to cross again.*'

I left my therapist's office for the last time. Judi had lost her objectivity, she had become emotionally involved and she had let me down. I had walked into her office, suicidally despondent and feeling horrific shame, and she had shamed me even more. *This was a psychologist?*

I never saw Judi again.

I called Bill at 9 p.m. on his cell phone, having discreetly gotten the number from Joseph's address book a while back. Bill was furious upon hearing my voice.

"I'm camping! I don't want to hear this!" he shouted and hung up on me. Angrily, I called him back and left my final message on his cell phone. As well, I wrote out the copy again and mailed it in case he deleted my voice message before he listened to it.

Bill was indeed a coward.

The harrowing aftermath of the reunion had shattered my life to pieces. For the next several days, I tried in vain to heal from the devastation.

I knew I couldn't survive much longer.

14 *Separation*

Five days had elapsed since Bill had left town.

Joseph was preparing to leave Calgary to move to Vancouver to live with Bill. He called me several times, wanting to borrow something. The sound of his voice alarmed me, and unable to speak to him, I let the answering machine record his messages. He unexpectedly dropped by with Becki and stood on the front porch, stubbornly ringing the doorbell. Cautiously, I peered out the window and saw that it was him. Terrified, I crouched down and hid behind a wall. Finally, to my relief, the two of them left.

My vacation was over. I wondered how in God's name I was going to face work the following day in the horrific state I was in. It was another miserable, sleepless night as I awoke throughout the night, screaming in terror.

Incredibly, I managed to arrive on time the first day back at work. I was extremely nervous and anxious and it was an immense struggle to get anything accomplished. I had completely lost my ability to focus and could not remember simple instructions. It was indeed a difficult time, and I could only pray that the day would end before I made a terrible mistake.

My son called when I got home, wanting to store his furniture. The sound of his voice triggered another anxiety attack, and after much deliberation, I called him back and left a firm message on his answering machine.

Joseph, the answer to your request is no. The answer to all further requests is no. Good luck in B.C. Good-bye! and I hung up. I couldn't allow him to use me again. Since meeting up with Bill, he had treated me as if I did not exist and had rarely spoken to me. Now that Billy Boy had left town, Joseph was back, expecting me to be there for him.

Later that same afternoon, Becki dropped by. I told her how Joseph had abused me for years and how I had given and given until I could give no more. Surprised, Becki said sweetly:

"I don't understand why you can't get along." Startled by her unsuspecting naiveté, I corrected her:

"Becki, it has nothing to do with getting along. Joseph has to change his attitude and treat me with respect. Until then, this relationship is finished. I can't do it anymore. Joseph's a very troubled young man, and he has taken all his anger out on me for years." Becki admitted that he still did that with her.

"Becki, I love my son very much and I'd give him the world, but that would leave nothing for me. I have nothing more to give." Becki was understanding and hugged me. I was indeed afraid for this beautiful, young woman standing in front of me.

"Becki, when your son makes you feel like you want to die, something has to change. A separation from Joseph will be a good thing for me because I need to heal from all the pain he has caused me.

I wept inconsolably, "Joseph is emotionally abusive, Becki. When Bill was here, Joseph shunned me and completely shut me out." Becki acknowledged that that must have hurt.

Miserably, I told her, "Joseph told me he would be on Bill's side all the way if I took Bill to court for money."

To my surprise, Becki said, "When you told him that, it made him very uncomfortable. Joey felt he would lose his father if you went after child support."

"Becki, child support was my right and none of Joe's business. What kind of man would Bill be if he dumped his son because I went after him for child support?" Becki agreed with me.

"Becki, Joseph has never given me any support or loyalty. Not even so much as saying, *'Mom, I'm on your side.'*" Becki was distressed hearing my words and spoke compassionately.

"He cares. I know he cares," she said fervently.

"Becki, he doesn't show it." We talked awhile longer and Becki left. Joey would be furious that I had revealed the truth about him to his girlfriend. Surely, it was my responsibility to warn her. I could not stand by and let her suffer what I had suffered.

Joseph was accepted at UBC for environmental engineering studies. Although I was happy he had been accepted and that he was going on to get a second degree, I was panic-stricken that he was leaving to live with Bill. I had heard of separation anxiety before, but this was far more complicated. Not only would I be separated from my son, but also he would be with people who had no respect for me and refused to acknowledge my existence. Under such circumstances, I could not possibly contact my son and would be completely cut off from him. Overcome with despair, I decided I had to speak to Bill and nervously dialed his number. My voice was strained and cracked with emotion as I left a desperate, tearful plea on his answering machine.

Bill, this is Maureen.

Joe has been accepted at UBC and will probably be leaving in two or three weeks to live out there.

I'm heartbroken, Bill, not only because he's leaving, but also because there has been so much animosity towards me by you and your wife. I'm afraid I won't be contacted in case of an emergency, and I'm afraid you will deny me telephone privileges with my son.

I love my son very much and I care what happens to him out there. So I'm pleading with you that we put any animosity aside for everyone's sake.

I apologize for saying I would never recognize you as his father. It was said out of anger. Please forgive me. Could you please call me at work or at home?

The day wore on and there was no phone call.

Needing support, I phoned a friend, Norma. She snapped irritably at me.

"You still haven't let go of your son! You overindulged him, and that's why he's still a kid and never grew up! If he had had a father, this wouldn't have happened. Your overindulgence is to blame for his immaturity. You're probably wishing it won't work out for him in B.C. You should be wishing them all happiness." I gasped in astonishment at her undeserved cruelty.

"Norma, you're being unfair. I have tried many times to stop my son's manipulations and selfishness, and after the way I have been treated by Bill and his girlfriend, I can hardly wish them all happiness." She continued to admonish me severely.

"Maureen, you're obsessed with all of this. You've babied your son, you've given him everything and you have to let him go." Hurt by Norma's biting words, I tried valiantly to defend myself.

"All I did was get him into sports. How is that everything?" Norma continued to reprimand me harshly, and I was relieved to get off the phone.

Ashamed and guilt-ridden by my friend's caustic scorn, I lay down on my bed and wept profusely. *Was this all my fault? Had I made my son become what he was?* I had done the best I could, and it wasn't my fault he didn't have a father. Nor did I give him everything as Norma had so unjustly accused me of doing. I only bought him what I could afford and paid for numerous sports and equipment. Wasn't that a healthy thing to do? How was that overindulgence? He had become a master manipulator, and I was powerless to stop it. It just wasn't in my character or nature to be aggressive, manipulative or dishonest, and I had had a very hard time fighting those unhealthy traits in my son. I had fought so hard, I couldn't fight any longer. The fight had simply gone out of me.

Certainly, I had tolerated my son's rage, and it was now time to let him go. It would be awhile before I fully understood that the '*one human being the most capable of curbing the anti-social aggression of a boy is his biological father.*'[4] Unfortunately, Bill was not capable of being a father to Joseph. He was simply too unhealthy and cared only for himself.

In any event, I knew I didn't deserve to be so horribly shamed by my friend and realized that our friendship was drawing to a close. Anyone who judged, scolded or emotionally abused me as she did could hardly be called a friend.

I continued to panic and cry over the pending loss of my son. Bill's refusal to speak to me or acknowledge me added to my already overwhelming anxiety. I was extremely weak, I ate very little and I was unable to sleep.

Finally, I got ahold of Joseph and was able to coax him into having dinner with me. I needed to spend a few quiet, peaceful hours with him before he left. He could conceivably be gone for the next four years and I didn't know when I would see him again.

We finally got together a few days later. He acted strangely and refused to look at me. I reminded him to make sure he put me as the legal next-of-kin on his school records so that they would call me in the event of a medical emergency. He didn't appear to be listening. We left for the restaurant in my car, and I reminded him that Bill was not his legal next-of-kin and could not sign for emergency surgery. To my dismay, Joseph berated me.

"You said some things to Becki. Don't do that again!"

I turned to him and calmly said, "I will not take orders from you. Nor will I take your guilts, your manipulations or your crap." He was furious with me.

"Do you know how you made Becki feel?"

I replied matter-of-factly, "You sent Becki over, and I had to explain to her why I wasn't storing your furniture. But wait a second— I don't have to explain or justify anything to you."

"It's too bad, Mom, that we couldn't get along before I leave."

I responded bluntly, "You can leave mad, you can leave sad— it really doesn't matter to me. I'm not taking your crap anymore."

"Let me out of the car!" he shouted.

"Sure, I'll drive you back." *So much for our farewell dinner.* We returned to my place and I wished him good luck out in B.C. He roared off in his truck, infuriated with me.

I was stunned, but at that moment, I really didn't care. I was sick of his admonishments, his belittlements, his disrespect and his disloyalty. I could not take any more. He was punishing me for revealing the truth about him to Becki—the truth she had never known.

The next day, I spoke to my good friend Julie. She urged me, "Leave Joey alone now. Don't phone him. Leave him be."

I spoke to another friend, Sue, and told her of my son treating me with scorn and disdain. She explained, "It's not about you. It's about himself." Instinctively, I knew Sue was right. My son had always needed constant approval and couldn't possibly feel good about himself.

Without my close friends, I would have been lost. They gave me unending comfort and support, and without them, I would not have survived the traumatic upheavals with my son.

Time was running out, and I needed to remind Joseph of happier times and of things we had done together throughout his life—things I didn't want him to forget. Tearfully, I wrote about my love for him and sent him the message by e-mail.

I spoke to Joseph the following day and told him that some day he would have to deal with the abandonment by Ernest and Bill in order to be happy inside, and he was unusually quiet. I asked him if he loved himself, and he answered, "Yes."

"Joseph, if you love yourself, then show some love for your Mom." I again asked him about our farewell dinner, and he insisted Becki come with us. I told him I needed time alone with him, but he refused unless Becki joined us. He was afraid of another fight. I pleaded with him to set a definite date, and he responded with an exasperating vagueness:

"We'll talk on the weekend."

"Joe, there's no more time!" He relented somewhat.

"Don't worry, Mom, we'll get together before I go."

I panicked. There was something different in his voice, and instinctively, I knew something was wrong. Frantically, I drove over to his place later that evening to find out what it was. Reluctantly, Joseph agreed to put aside his studying for a few minutes to walk around the block with me. He was strangely cold and aloof. When I questioned him, he shouted with rage:

"Grandma said you fucked Bill! Bill's mom said you fucked him! You knew all these years Bill was my father! You've lied to me all these years!" Reeling, I staggered back a few steps and gaped at him in disbelief.

"Joseph, what are you saying? I didn't know any such thing!"

Relentlessly, he insisted I knew all along Bill was his father. He chastised me for fighting with my mother and brother and told me I should make up with them.

I protested, "That's not your issue! I want people in my life that love me and treat me with respect!" He was combative and mercilessly attacked me again and again.

"Mom, I was going along just fine until you dragged me into all this mess!" he yelled. I told him it wasn't easy on me either.

"You did it for yourself—not for me!"

Shocked, I asked him incredulously, "What did I get out of it? I didn't even get closure!"

"You put me through hell the past two years! You're emotional and nervous!"

"Joseph, I never knew Bill was your father. Bill would never have stuck around—he would have run faster than anyone." To my amazement, Joseph agreed.

"No, he would have run—most guys would have."

"Joseph, I was just a young girl trying to survive with a tiny baby. The last thing I could have dealt with was the possibility that someone else could have been your father. It had to wait until Mom could actually see the resemblance between you and Bill. Don't you understand that?"

After twenty minutes of arguing, I finally managed to calm him down and gave him a couple of hugs and told him I loved him. There were tears in his eyes as I said good-bye and walked back to my car. I was traumatized and shaken by his contemptuous and cruel attack. I had never seen him seething with such uncontrollable rage and aggressiveness, and it scared me.

The next day, after worrying and troubling over Joseph's allegations, I sent him another e-mail.

Joseph, this is after our conversation at your place. I need to clarify a few things.

I have a recorded conversation with Ernest dated March, 1995 wherein he confirmed that I was a virgin when it first happened.

I have your birth records stating the EDC (Expected Date of Confinement or Due Date) was the end of November. You were born the end of October.

Obviously, you were not born early; you were born on time because I was with Bill three weeks prior to Ernest. Bill was perhaps a very inexperienced young man and may not have realized that he didn't get to third base.

Bill, Laurie and you wanted me out of it. So I am. I want nothing more to do with it. I wish you and them the best.

Love, Mom

I would be relieved when Joseph finally left. I was incapable of tolerating any more abuse from him than I already had. I had hung in there for as long as I could. Any more, and it would undoubtedly cost me my life.

It was Monday and I called Joseph to remind him of our farewell dinner that evening. He procrastinated again.

"Maybe Wednesday."

"Okay, keep Wednesday open. Bye, sweetie."

Two days later I felt a sudden compulsion to speak to Elizabeth in the office. She was a kind and gentle soul and was aware of all the trouble I had been having with my son. She listened intently as I tearfully recounted the latest emotional turmoil with Joseph.

"Maureen, I know of a doctor that I used to see. He's a wonderful man and he helped me immensely. Why don't you go see him?"

Bewildered, I asked her, "Why would I want to see a doctor?" *There's nothing wrong with me.* She told me he had helped her through a difficult time and that perhaps he could help me.

Back at my desk, the tears started afresh. Perhaps Elizabeth was right—perhaps I did need to see a doctor. The escalating panic, confusion and anxiety was not going away. I typed up a summary detailing the events of the past twenty-four months as well as my accompanying symptoms and made an appointment for later that day.

Dr. Narsui was indeed a wonderful man. I sat and wept while he read my summary. He was compassionate and kind and spoke gently to me.

"Maureen, you cannot expect people to treat you as you would treat them. These are not healthy people." I cried, hearing his words. He continued, "Maureen, your son cannot handle your emotions because it fills him with fear. Joseph needs to see you as the solid rock you have always been before this. He will continue to dump on you because he does not know the people out there in B.C. He will not dump on them at all." I groaned in dismay.

"You are the one he loves, and he dumps on you because he knows and trusts you. He knows you will never leave him. Just understand why he does it, because he will do it again." His words were comforting.

"Maureen, you are suffering from severe clinical depression, and you should have been treated with a mild anti-depressant at least six months ago." I was heartened, hearing that there was a medical name for what I was suffering. *Clinical depression. Why hadn't I seen it?*

"Maureen, you have been hurt badly, and your body has been severely stressed. The serotonin levels in your body have crashed from the chronic stress and that is why you have been unable to recover and why therapy isn't working. Your condition is not a psychological one, but rather a medical one. Therapy should always be used in conjunction with medicine."

I responded morosely, "Dr. Narsui, I don't want to go back to therapy. It wasn't helping, and my therapist shamed me badly, telling me that '*I had really done a number on myself.*'" Dr. Narsui wanted to know my psychologist's name and wrote it in my record.

"Maureen, I'm giving you some pills, and I want you to take one right away and go out and have a nice supper with your son tonight. Come back and see me tomorrow for a chat."

"Dr. Narsui—that's impossible! Even the thought of my son makes me cry!" His voice was conciliatory.

"Maureen, you're going to be okay. Go to dinner. Everything's going to be okay." I continued to weep and asked him how could that possibly be? He repeated soothingly, "You're going to be fine at dinner. Go and enjoy it, and come back and see me tomorrow and tell me all about it."

I took the pill as he instructed and left his office. Two hours passed and I began to feel a little strange. Tears came to my eyes, but they disappeared almost immediately. I was finally able to control the desperate crying. Incredibly, I decided I could handle dinner after all. I was immensely grateful that Elizabeth had recommended Dr. Narsui. He was indeed a wonderful man—a very kind and caring, intelligent and spiritual man.

Joseph called, and for the first time in six months, I was able to speak to him without crying. He sounded stressed. I told him to meet me at my house and that I had a gift for him—an early birthday present. Joseph was pleased with the cobalt-blue towels I bought him.

We had a lovely dinner at Earl's, and I told him that I had been diagnosed with depression. He was surprised but didn't say too much. After dinner we picked Becki up, and the three of us went for a long walk through the paths at Edworthy Park. Not only had it become a place of solace for me, but also Joseph himself had ridden the trails many times as a youngster. I felt contented to finally spend a few peaceful moments with him. I had waited so long for this. Arm in arm, we walked along the trail, enjoying each other's company. At one point, Joseph remarked:

"You can pay my way home for Christmas." I hesitated, unable to speak. Becki corrected him:

"No, Joey, you pay your own way home." I was relieved Becki spoke up for me because I really didn't have the energy to speak up for myself. I was utterly worn out from all the fighting. I asked Joseph if he would be home for Christmas, and he promised me he would. After a long, enjoyable walk, I took the two of them to Dairy Queen for a treat.

Back at the house, I told Becki that Joseph and I still had things to work out in our relationship, but that it was happening and that his leaving was a good thing—that we needed the separation from each other. I told her that her relationship with him would get better, and she frowned.

"No, I don't think so." I assured her it would grow stronger, and she shook her head sadly, 'No.'

"Becki, trust me on this one. He's finally starting to feel his emotions. His love will grow stronger. It will be a pure love, but he needs to go away to learn some hard lessons and to mature and grow. Then he can come back and be able to really love. Your relationship with him will improve and so will mine. Trust me on this one." Becki was not convinced.

"I'm afraid Joey will turn into a seventeen-year-old out there." I knew she was referring to Bill and Joey drinking in the bars. She was worried and I assured her that that wouldn't happen.

After they left, I was up all night, unable to sleep. I went back to see Dr. Narsui the following day, and he told me that 'that was normal.'

"Maureen, you'll be up for three nights in a row. It's your body getting used to the medication." I was shocked. He was reluctant to give me sleeping pills but said he could give me half a sleeping pill for each of the next two nights. I told him I would rather do that than stay up for 72 hours. Amazingly, the little half a pill worked wonderfully and put me to sleep very gently that night. For the first time in two years, I slept soundly.

I had not yet regained my appetite and discovered I had lost 30 pounds. I was still extremely weak from the chronic lack of sleep and found myself crying because my son was leaving. I realized the anti-depressant pills didn't mask real emotions but only controlled the depressive symptoms. I took another half a sleeping pill the following evening and again slept well.

It was Saturday and Joseph and Becki unexpectedly dropped by while I was sleeping. I got up and made lunch for them and we sat in the backyard. It was a lovely, sunny afternoon. Joe discussed his trip and said he was leaving Wednesday night after work.

Sunday came and I was depressed and weeping. Joseph called

me and I told him I was having a hard time accepting that he was leaving. He invited me to his place for dinner and I brought fresh corn for Becki. I felt so sick, I barely ate. Discouraged, I helped Joseph pack up boxes in the garage. Although I felt it was a big mistake—him packing up lock, stock and barrel to move out to B.C. to live with Bill—I kept my thoughts to myself. It would only fuel another fight. Joseph was arrogant and spoke disparagingly to me.

"Did you call Bill when you were upset? Why did you do that?" *How did he know that and why was it any of his business?* I was frank with him.

"Yes, I called Bill and asked that the animosity stop."

"Mom, Laurie told me that you had called Bill and that you were very distraught. She wanted me to reassure you that you can call there anytime." *So that's how it worked. I call Bill, Bill tells Laurie, Laurie tells Joey and Joey tells me. Talk about effective communication, I thought wryly.* I defended myself.

"I had a reason to be upset because Bill hung up on me when I asked him about a meeting. Also, I was concerned they wouldn't let me speak to you."

"When did you call Bill?" he asked suspiciously.

"I called Bill after he left Calgary to ask him why he didn't keep his promise of a meeting with me. You do realize that's why I'm suffering from depression? Because of the way these people treated me?" He answered impassively:

"Yes, I realize that, but I didn't want to get involved." *How many times had I heard him say that? So what if your Mom's suicidally depressed—all the more reason not to get involved?*

"Fine. But at least validate me and tell me you're on my side." He acknowledged that he was, but I knew I could no longer trust my son.

"Why wouldn't Bill meet with me?" I asked him sadly.

"I guess he can't face his past," Joseph answered. I told my son that sooner or later, Bill would have to face his past.

After three hours of helping Joey sort and pack his stuff, I left and told him I would drop by Tuesday night to say good-bye. He grudgingly said okay.

I woke up the next morning, sick as a dog, and missed work. I slept the day away and decided that I had had enough. I spoke to Becki later that evening and told her I wouldn't be dropping by the following evening after all.

"Becki, it would just be too painful and stressful," I told her sadly.

"You'll see him at the airport anyway," she said comfortingly.

"No, Becki, seeing Joey off at the airport would be too much for me right now. My health is suffering, I haven't eaten for several days and I have to take care of myself. It was stressful seeing Joey on Sunday, and I was so sick that I missed work today. I can't take any more stress." Becki agreed that I had to take care of myself. I told her I would just phone Joey to say good-bye instead of dropping by.

It was Tuesday night. Joseph phoned and asked if I was coming over.

"No, honey, I can't. I've been through too much already and it would just be too painful for me." He said he would call the next day before he left.

"Why don't we just say good-bye now?" I sighed wearily. I told him I loved him and to call me when he got to Vancouver. For the first time in a very long time, he was nice to me. I told him I would miss him, and he said he would miss me as well. I got off the phone and wept. *My baby's leaving tomorrow.*

Finally, Wednesday arrived. Joseph called me at work and asked me to deposit his cheques for him.

"Mom, I'm scared," he said apprehensively.

"Joseph, you'll be fine. I love you! I love you more than anything! Take care, son."

He responded warmly with an, "I love you too."

The struggle was over. The battle had been valiantly fought and tragically lost. Although I loved my son deeply, it was now time to love and heal myself. I was taking the following week off from work, and hopefully I would begin recovery from what had been a horrendously painful journey to hell. I was thankful the anti-depressant medication was beginning to restore my balance, finally.

I thought about my son. Joseph and Becki had decided to drive out to Vancouver and would be there late the following evening. *God, watch over my son and keep him safe from harm. Good-bye my son, for now. I love you more than all the universes!*

Once again, I cried the night away.

15 *Recovery*

A month passed. Recovery had finally begun.

On the instructions of Dr. Narsui, a psychiatric assessment and counseling sessions began at the Psychiatric Unit of the Foothills Hospital. Although initially unnerved at the prospect of returning to a place I remembered only too well from my troubled youth, I realized it was a necessary and vital part of my recovery. I cried my way through weeks of counseling, not giving a damn about who was observing me behind the curtained window.

The psychiatric assessment was complete. I was diagnosed with not one, but two, debilitating mental illnesses—severe clinical depression and a generalized anxiety disorder. I was to continue seeking treatment through my doctor. Concerned over the diagnosis, I spoke to the Chief Psychiatrist.

"Maureen, anyone who has suffered prolonged, extreme stress as you, would have ended up in a major depression. I would like you to seek further counseling for the unresolved birthright issue with a psychologist or psychiatrist who specializes in that field." Unfortunately, he knew of no such person himself and was unable to help me further.

I left the hospital for the last time. It felt good, knowing I was finally being taken care of.

Joseph continued to telephone every day from B.C. leaving

messages on my phone. Finally, after much deliberation, I decided to speak to him. He was angry. "Why haven't you been returning my messages?" he demanded to know.

"Joe, I have been ill—very ill." He grunted in response. I asked him how he was.

He grumbled, "Vancouver's too big and busy. Laurie's daughter moved home—she's a real bitch, and it's too crowded in the house." There was an awkward pause. "So how's school?" I asked quietly. He complained even louder.

"It's hard and different and there's no place to study in the house—it's so noisy. Everyone gets up in the morning, yelling at each other and making a lot of racket."

Somewhat wearily, I asked him how work was going.

"I have too many hours at work. And I have to take the bus everywhere. Do you know how big Vancouver is?" I was silent. There was a long pause. Finally, Joseph spoke.

"If it doesn't work out, I'll just come home." I was aghast at the idea of him returning home so soon and asked him about Laurie and Bill. He responded that they were fine.

"Has Bill or Laurie ever mentioned my name?" I asked tediously, to which Joe replied, "No."

"So Bill and Laurie pushed me out of everything and pretend I don't exist, I'm sitting here diagnosed with severe depression and you think everything is fine?" I asked incredulously.

"According to Bill and Laurie, it is." I started to cry and told him everything was not fine. "Mom, don't worry—everything will be just fine."

Morosely, I asked, "How? These people pretend I don't exist. How can you say everything's fine?"

Loftily, he invited me for Christmas. "Where would I stay, Joseph?"

Laughing, he answered, "Well, here, at Laurie and Bill's."

Exasperated with him, I cried, "Joe, these people don't even talk to me. How could I stay for Christmas?"

He countered, "So what! Stay here anyway." Frustrated with

his obnoxious attitude, I told him I had to go and hung up. He had only called to vent his frustrations and couldn't be bothered to ask how I was. It was another miserable night, and the following day, sick with anxiety and overwhelming despondency, I stayed in bed. It was a stupid mistake, speaking to my son.

Joseph continued calling and the sound of his voice triggered further alarming anxiety attacks. Finally, I told him of my counseling sessions at the hospital and the diagnosis. "I have you and the rest of them to thank for this, Joseph." Emphatically, he denied having done anything wrong.

"I want one hell of an apology before I can ever forgive you, and until then, don't bother me again!" We shouted at each other, and I slammed the phone down on his ear.

In desperation, I phoned the woman at the adoption agency once again and told her that I needed to speak to someone immediately about the birthright issue—that my situation had ended up very badly. She was very sympathetic.

"Maureen, we don't have the experience to deal with your situation. Try Colleen Clark at *Imagine*. Colleen has far more expertise in this area. I think she would be a good person to talk to."

I managed to get ahold of Colleen and made an appointment with her for later that evening. When I entered the building where Colleen maintained her practice, I was startled by an odd sensation of going back in time. Incredibly, it was the same building I used to go to to fight for child support cheques when my son was a child. I had indeed come full circle.

After being introduced to Colleen, I was led to a small, comfortable room. I gave her a copy of my summary to read while I sat quietly across from her and waited patiently. When she had finished, we spent the next two hours talking.

"Maureen, everything in your life you thought was—wasn't! Only you know what you have been through, and you have been through major, major trauma. I understand because I specialize in trauma. Your life as you knew it is no more. You have torn all the skeletons out of the closet—all in one big bang. You have touched your very soul!" I cried in anguish at her words. *Finally, someone understood.* She continued:

"Maureen, you have an identity for the first time in your life. For the first time in your life, you're going to be a whole, complete person, and for the first time in your life, you are free." We talked about Bill, and she confirmed that I needed to see Bill for closure and pointed out something important.

"You also needed to make this real. It isn't real yet to you."

"Colleen, I'm still in the fantasy and it hurts." She confirmed my feelings and explained:

"You also needed to see Bill to understand and see your son's identity." Perplexed, I asked Colleen why Bill and Laurie refused to acknowledge my existence.

She responded emphatically, "These people, by denying you exist, are denying your identity. They are denying your son's identity as well. Your son is living a lie, denying his own identity. These people are living in the lies, and you are in the truth. Stay in the truth!" I wept with relief. Finally, I was getting answers from someone who knew exactly what was going on.

"Colleen, Joseph has tried to call me 40-45 times, and I haven't answered."

Colleen observed, "You have created a crisis situation out there." Confused, I asked her if I had done anything wrong.

"No! By not answering his calls, you are forcing him to face this situation and deal with it himself. Perhaps he'll finally grow up." Colleen paused reflectively. "That's why your son has called you 45 times. He's saying, *'I have an identity—I have a mother.'*" Her next words stunned me.

"Maureen, you're re-enacting what happened in your family of origin all over again with Bill. Just as your family denied your identity, so has Bill, and it has triggered all the old family identity issues. You're saying to Bill, *'Look—I'm here! Here I am!'* By denying your identity, they have involved your son in secrecy and lies. It is wrong and unhealthy." She then prompted me:

"Maureen, what do you know about crisis?" Without hesitation, I answered:

"That it nearly kills you!" She smiled knowingly and repeated the question, and I answered her in the same way. Later, it would become evident to me what Colleen had wanted me to see. *Crisis is an opportunity for change and growth as one's world—one's reality—is shattered.*

"Maureen, you have drawn a line in the sand, and the worst thing you could do would be to answer your son's calls. It's time for him to face this situation alone. It is, after all, exactly what he wanted."

She spoke decisively. "Maureen, you are Bill's worst nightmare. You are your family's worst nightmare. You are your mother's worst nightmare. These people are all living in denial, and you are in the truth. Tell me—how did it feel when you told each family member to fuck off?"

I responded candidly, "Colleen, it felt good!"

She explained, "That's because you finally got your power back from them." Still confused, I asked her sadly:

"Colleen, how can Bill face his son and not me?" Once again, Colleen answered with an uncanny conviction and insight:

"Bill feels that because this is his son, he has a connection with him." I felt a wave of incredible relief. Finally, I understood. Bill thought that because he was Joseph's biological father and shared a few genes with him, there was an automatic connection or bond with his son. I couldn't help wondering with amazement: *Surely, connection is borne out of years of loving, caring and nurturing someone.*

"Maureen, as a therapist, I would never have advised your son to move in with Bill out there." I agreed with Colleen and told her I felt my son had made a big mistake, but in retrospect, perhaps it was a good thing—he would finally learn.

Colleen noted, "You gave your son everything you didn't have, including a father," to which I tearfully replied, "Yes, and it nearly killed me."

"Maureen, there will be a crisis out there very soon. The honeymoon is probably already over." I told Colleen that over a year ago I already knew I would be left out of the reunion. She looked at me strangely and asked:

"Maureen, what else do you know?" I looked at her and smiled. Her words were comforting and insightful. "Maureen, trust yourself. You are always right."

"Colleen, I lost control of the situation when I gave my son Bill's phone number. It will always hurt, Colleen, that I never got to see the two of them hug for the first time." I broke down and wept in heart wrenching despair. Colleen agreed that Joseph had betrayed me and what he did was very wrong.

"Colleen, why did I have to do all the suffering? No one else did." Her answer was definitive.

"Maureen, this was about you and your life! If Bill doesn't face things, he will probably end up depressed as well. Bill and Laurie are both very unhealthy people." There was a long pause. In a gentle voice, she asked:

"Maureen, do you hate Bill?" Once again, I started to cry and, unable to speak, sadly shook my head, 'No.'

Astutely, she asked, "Because he's your son's father?"

I managed to answer weakly, "Yes. I just can't hate him." There was an unparalleled certainty in Colleen's voice when she next spoke.

"Maureen, I believe there is a plan. This had to happen this way so that you would finally be strong enough to stand up to your son. All you did was overcompensate in bringing him up, but you did the best you could."

"I was a good mother, Colleen. I loved him so much," I cried sorrowfully.

"Sit back, Maureen, and watch everything unfold. Keep writing in your journal." Confidently, she affirmed, "It's not over until it's over. And this isn't over."

The session was finished and I left, reeling from the extraordinary knowledge Colleen not only possessed, but also shared with me. She was truly a woman of remarkable courage, character and wisdom and possessed an incredible awareness of the trauma of reunification and the complexity of birthright issues. I was acutely aware that it would be Colleen who would pull me through the black, seemingly endless, tunnel I had been hopelessly stuck in for over two years.

Two weeks passed and I saw Colleen again. We discussed the years of abuse my son had put me through. "Colleen, I've set a boundary and I can't back down on it."

"Maureen, what would make you want to back down on it? The boundaries have been building for a long time, and the reality is— Joe may never apologize—" Exasperated, I interrupted her.

"But he does apologize, eventually. And then the abuse starts all over again. This time, it's different though—I feel it's different—because this time, I'm different."

"Okay. So what's the difference with you now than say one year ago or three years ago?"

Tearfully, I replied, "The difference with me now is that I'm finally strong enough to stand up to him. Previously, I thought I'd lose him or I'd lose his love if I didn't phone him within a week or two after we had a fight. I would say to him, *'You're all I have!'* and I would start to cry."

"Maureen, can you look at the difference at who you are now from who you were then? *'You're the only thing I have'* sounds like a fear of abandonment to me."

"I was afraid he would leave me, Colleen!" I wailed in distress. Colleen spoke with a forceful assurance, and her words possessed beauty, strength, wisdom and compassion that could only have come from years of dedication and experience.

"Yes, but there has been a shift and a change, and you are probably more the functioning parent now than you have ever been because you're probably now more whole than you have ever been. Maureen, the biggest fear we can have is the fear of being rejected and not loved. You have not been loved the way you have needed to be loved."

"Colleen, I was afraid he would abandon me, so I would always say, *'Come on, let's get back together. Let's not fight.'*"

"But meanwhile, the pain inside of you didn't go away," she stressed compassionately.

"Colleen, I've been doing that for years with him. And he got worse, to the point where he was unmanageable. And if I didn't do exactly as he said—" I was too distraught to continue.

"So who controlled the relationship?" she asked gently.

"He did, Colleen! He controlled the relationship!" My body contorted in terribly agony. The realization was so very hard to bear. Colleen sat quietly, understanding my pain.

"Colleen, we clung to each other and I needed the break, but I didn't know how to do it."

"Maureen, things were the way they were because they needed to be like that. Things are different now—you are different."

Miserably, I cried, "So many times I just couldn't keep that boundary. Because I loved him, and after a week went by, I would miss him so much—and he knew it! He knew it!"

"Sure he knew it," she sympathized.

"When I didn't do exactly as he wanted me to do, he withdrew his love and wouldn't speak to me. He would punish me." There was a long silence.

"Maureen, what do you think is going to happen out there?" I struggled to regain a semblance of composure.

"Colleen, I'm worried. If everything is really good out there, Joseph is not going to change. I'll have the same son that I've always had, who has been so abusive to me. If he gets everything he wants out there, as he did with me, I've lost!" I sobbed unrelentingly as Colleen reassured me:

"Maureen, this relationship with them—it's just that. It's a new relationship. You have got your whole life with him. You have got the years spent with him that they will never have."

I replied matter-of-factly, "Bill didn't deserve it. He knew all along anyway, so he didn't deserve it." My voice rose in anger and I nearly shouted at poor Colleen:

"Colleen, every time I dropped the ball, my son manipulated me to keep me going! He would say, '*Wouldn't it be nice if I worked out there and Bill and his wife came into the store and Bill saw me and recognized me as his son?*' Every time I dropped the ball, Joseph was always there with another manipulative comment to guilt me so I would continue."

"So he was playing with you. And you can now identify the patterns."

"Oh, Colleen! He manipulates—" I stumbled in confusion and despair. "In fact, now I'm thinking back, and I wonder what he has said to my family over the years. I'm wondering if he isn't the one who has told my family I'm crazy. I'm starting to think of all these things and I'm thinking: *What has he done behind my back?*"

"You're questioning your trust for him," Colleen submitted.

"Oh, I have no trust for him now. Throughout this whole thing, he colluded with Laurie behind my back. And he hadn't even met her yet. That's a trustful son? I've been with him for twenty-four years—" My voice broke with unbearable pain. There was yet another long silence, interrupted only by the sounds of my suffering.

"What is your biggest fear?" Colleen asked quietly.

"I'm afraid that that relationship with Bill is going to turn out great. And I know that sounds bad. But I am."

"And what would that mean for you?" Confused, I groped for an answer.

"I don't know. I think it leaves me nowhere with Joseph because he would have got what he wanted. And how do I accept it if it does turn out wonderful? How do I accept that? Somebody once said to me, *'You've got to wish them well and wish them all happiness.'* Well, I don't feel that way, Colleen. I don't feel that way."

"And how come you don't?" she asked gently.

"Because they nearly destroyed me through this! How can I turn around and wish them happiness?"

Colleen confirmed, "Because they caused you so much pain through this process, where there didn't need to be this pain."

"Yes, that's right! And I'm angry! I'm angry that that had to happen! I'm angry that I had to end up with a severe depression and an anxiety disorder and a functioning level of 40%. Sure, I've got my power back and I'm taking medication, but I'm angry that I went through all that pain. And I don't know how to let go of all that. I don't know how."

Colleen maintained, "Because they're not going to understand your pain or what it has been like for you to raise a son on your own or all the other things that were going on in your family."

"They don't care!" I cried. "Neither does my son!" Colleen nodded her head in quiet agreement.

"No, they're not going to get it," I agreed sadly. "Colleen, I'm embarrassed and ashamed of how my son has treated me through this. I'm so ashamed of him. And if he gets in good with Bill—Bill is—he's going to be just like Bill. Bill is just like Joey. They're like each other!" I cried frantically.

"And that's one of your fears," Colleen surmised.

"Bill is just like him. I think Joey is just like his father, in a sense."

"Emotionally? Or in what way?" she asked.

"Never accepting responsibility for what he's done. How can I have a relationship with my son when he denies anything he has ever said or done to hurt me?" I asked skeptically.

"Well, it's hard. That makes you question what your reality is—what is real and what isn't real."

"But I know it's real. I don't forget the things he has said." My voice tremored with an overwhelming sadness.

"Colleen, this whole thing is a mess, and I'm terrified to see my son because I don't want to. And that scares me."

"So not only are you questioning your relationship with him, but also wondering if you want to see him." She pondered for a few moments. "Maureen, not only were you a single parent, but also you now have the added dynamic of the birth father."

"Now I have got to deal with Bill having his influence on my son!" I cried in alarm.

"But you have never had that added dynamic before because you were basically Mom, Dad—you name it—you were it. It's almost like Joey's going back to being a child on some level. On one level he's an adult who has left home, and if he had just left home from your home, it would have been okay."

"Colleen, I'm okay that he left. If he were just out in Vancouver, I'd be fine with that, but that's not the case. And going back to his childhood, you're right about that. Because when he was going out there he said, *'Bill promised me money and promised me help through university,'* and I thought: *Oh great!*"

Colleen wisely observed, "So what he's done is he's living a fantasy in order to re-create something he didn't have as a child—which is having a father. And it will crash. Reality will set in. Trust my words on this."

"Colleen, if it doesn't crash, it's a worse situation. Bill still goes to the bar—he never grew up. He still acts like a child. He's not a father."

"Maureen, you have no power or control over that. You have raised your son the best way you could."

"And I instilled a lot of values in him."

"Of course you did. They are there, somewhere," she agreed.

"I wonder if he's not more like Bill."

"Well, right now he's probably wanting to identify with Bill. His pull might be so strong to have a father figure, he's probably created a fantasy father figure."

"He has!" I agreed emphatically.

"Of course he has. And that is very normal when you're dealing with identity issues and when you're dealing with kids who don't know who their parent has been. They will re-create whatever they need to cope and survive." She explained further:

"And probably one of the most difficult processes that happens when you do reunify is letting go of the fantasy. That's when you hit the ground with two feet. It is probably one of the biggest losses to deal with—the reality that this person is a human being. And that can take time to check it all out."

"I don't think it will take Joey too long," I told her.

"Well, he's very bright," Colleen agreed. "Maureen, he's assuming that if it doesn't work out there, he gets to come home to you. The question is this: Is that one of your realities?"

"That he can come back to me?" I asked.

"Yes. This is about boundaries. This is about what you need."

"I think if I rescued him in that respect, I don't think it would help us any, Colleen."

"I agree with that. I can understand the emotional need to say *'Good! Come back to me!'* That would be the rescuer. But wait a second. What is this about? This is about boundaries. I'm not going to have you talk to me like that. I am your mother. I've raised you the best way that I can. Maureen, the answers have to come to this: What do you want?"

"Colleen, I just need respect from him, and I need for him to stop blaming me. He got what he wanted. Maybe I was jealous because I was left out of all of this. Jealous and very, very hurt!"

"And that's okay to say that you were jealous and very hurt. You should be hurt. And you should be jealous. Those are normal, healthy feelings to have, based on the situation. It's like—here you are—and the white knight comes rescuing Joey. Where was Bill all those years? You have a right to be angry and hurt."

"He didn't want to be in his son's life. And Joey has not accepted that."

"Okay. So I think Joey is in a part of denial where you are getting all his anger. Would his father have come searching for him? I doubt it."

"No! Oh no! Bill had all those years—he knew I was in Calgary."

"Probably not too hard to find," Colleen surmised.

"I wouldn't have been hard to find at all. Colleen, Joey wants to identify with Bill so damned bad, he's got to agree with what Bill did." Colleen agreed and reassured me firmly:

"Maureen, you are his mother. No one can ever take that away."

"I feel like it has been taken away!" I wept in excruciating pain. "Colleen, I didn't have a father. Why, why was it so important for my son? Because he's a male? A lot of us grow up without fathers."

"Is it okay though?" she asked gently.

"But we accept it," I countered.

"But is it okay?" she challenged.

"No, I don't think it's okay," I answered resignedly.

"I agree. It's not okay."

"Well, now that I have set that boundary, I don't want to phone him, Colleen. He just doesn't get it."

"No. So who does get it?" Colleen pressed.

"I get it. He doesn't get it. He'll never—"

"Maybe he won't get it. Or maybe he's not as wise as you are, yet. Life is going to be his greatest teacher, if he chooses to learn. You have done the best you could. As mothers, we can only give our children the best that we can do at that time. The reality is he has left home. You have done your job. Look at what you have given him: safety, security, stability—" I interrupted Colleen.

"Direction, values, I helped him with his goals, I gave him nurturing, love—"

"Okay! So you have given him the foundation," Colleen assured me.

"Yes, I did."

"And probably at a cost to you that he will never understand, nor will anyone else because they weren't there. Nor will they understand the pain of being a single parent and not having enough food or not knowing what you're doing with your life and saying, *'This is it?'* Look at the sacrifice. You have done your job. Maureen, I think you need to stop and look at this. You need to grieve that he is now gone. Forget where he's gone to—that's a whole other intensity."

"I'm okay that he's gone, Colleen. Part of me does miss him, and I cry once in a while about that, but I'm okay that he's out there because I knew he had to be away from me."

"Okay. So you knew that," she confirmed.

"Oh, yes! I knew I had to get the hell away from him too, to heal!" I exclaimed passionately.

"Maureen, time is the determining factor in all of life. Things will unfold in time if we get out of the way—if we get out of our own way."

"I miss him, Colleen," I cried tearfully. Her words were

consoling.

"It's okay to miss him. It's okay to love him. It's okay to write him and talk about your boundaries and your love for him. Nobody can take away you being a loving person. That's one of the gifts you have. You don't have to hate him."

"No, I can't hate him," I said sadly.

"I think that even hurts you more when you try to because that goes against who you are. You are not a hateful person. But you also have a right to be respected. You also have a right to say what you need too. We all do." She continued:

"Maureen, Joseph cannot meet your expectations right now. He's not there. He has not done the degree of work you have done. He has to acknowledge how badly he has treated you. You need to get an apology for what he has done. There's stuff going on right now and he wants to save face. This is his biggest fantasy come true—meeting his birth father and living with him. Life will teach him what he needs to know. And for the first time in your life, you get to be free ... We can go back, Maureen, but you need to question whether or not you want to. The cost is going to be too high. You are an amazing woman, Maureen."

I didn't feel so amazing.

And I had a strange, foreboding sense that it was not yet over.

16 *Integration*

Unexpectedly, Joseph arrived in town for the weekend.

Horrified at the mere prospect of seeing my son, I cowered and hid in a darkened house and bolted to the window at the sound of every car that drove by. I peered anxiously out the narrow slats of the window blinds and kept several hours' grueling vigil. Nervously, I checked and re-checked the front and back door locks, afraid Joseph would break in. Finally, utterly exhausted, I succumbed to a deeply troubled sleep. A nightmarish blur of gruesome sensations and frightening images awakened me throughout the night, screaming in terror.

I had suffered too much trauma. The damage had been done.

Relentlessly, Joseph called and left a stream of messages on my answering machine. The sound of his voice distressed me profoundly, and in desperation, I finally told him:

"Joseph, I told you the last time we spoke, and I've told you again and again—I need a sincere apology for all the pain you have caused me and an acknowledgment of all the things you have done to hurt me." He groaned, then laughed and sneered with contempt:

"And I've told you again and again that I feel there's nothing I need to apologize for."

"Then there's nothing more for us to talk about. Good-bye."

Distraught that nothing had changed, I sent Joseph a very harsh e-mail and told him that he no longer controlled me or any relationship with me and that the game was over.

The sessions with Colleen continued while I struggled to integrate the shattered pieces of my life. Colleen had lent me a book to read at the close of our last session. *The Primal Wound* dealt with reunifications of adoptees and birth parents, the parallels of which were remarkably identical to those I had so painfully and disastrously suffered. My voice tremored with overwhelming emotion as I read a meaningful passage from the book to her.

"Reunions can indeed be a vital part of the healing process for all sides of the [adoption] triad. But for healing to take place, all must own their own feelings as well as acknowledge and accept those of the others. No one can be left out because each has been a part of the process. Each needs to stop projecting and passing judgment and instead provide understanding and support for one another."

"Basically, Colleen, that says it all to me."

"Basically, you are the only one who has been open and willing to explore," she affirmed.

"I should have been involved, Colleen!"

"Oh yes! But you always knew that," she assured me unequivocally.

"But I couldn't make anyone else see that. Bill's girlfriend had no right to exclude me—this wasn't her issue." Colleen nodded her head in silent agreement.

"Maureen, how did it make you feel, reading the book? Did it make you feel validated? Sad?" she asked gently. A tormented cry escaped my lips and I wailed in profound anguish:

"I don't know that I'm ever going to get over this! I don't want to see my son for a very long time!"

"You're feeling angry, Maureen? Because when you read something like that, it can make everything more concrete, more real."

"Colleen, a lot of people didn't understand what I was feeling or why."

"Maureen, a lot of people aren't aware of the dynamics involved in the process of reunification. It's one of the most complicated areas of psychology that I have seen in clinical practice. Many people shut down emotionally because dealing with the reality of a situation is too intense. You were not dealing with people who were capable of handling the situation."

"Colleen, I didn't know the professional—clinical—end of it, but I felt it. I knew I belonged in the reunion. I don't know if I can ever forgive him for that."

Tearfully, I managed to recite a second passage from *The Primal Wound* to Colleen.

"Someone ends up being labeled the bad guy. The anger and frustration which are triggered by many aspects of the [adoption] process need an outlet—an external target. Unfortunately for everyone concerned, that target is often some member of the triad itself."

I was unable to continue.

"And you're it! So in a way, a lot of what is happening is classic, predictable."

"Everything was taken out on me!" I cried miserably. Colleen spoke with authority and conviction.

"Maureen, it sounds like things have been taken out on you for a long time, beginning with your family of origin. You have been the scapegoat. People have looked at you to blame and to be angry at. But you have also been Miss Dependable. What's happening now is that those roles aren't working for you anymore."

"Colleen, in the search for the truth, I let a lot of things go including my son's anger at me because I knew this was a traumatic thing for him as well. That gave him indescribable power over me the last two years."

"But it sounds like he's had power over you for a long time, Maureen," Colleen said knowingly.

"Yes, but for the last two years, it was far greater than it ever was." I paused reflectively. "So reading that book was good for me."

"Was it pretty painful to read?" she asked quietly. My voice quivered with unutterable sadness.

"Yes, because I'm the one with the primal wound. My son was okay. He even yelled at me one time, '*I was fine until you dragged me into all this mess!* But I knew he needed to see his father or meet his father to feel whole and complete. I knew that—I felt it."

Colleen's words were uttered with a skillful and compelling summation of the truth.

"Maureen, through this process you gave your son this gift, but you have also given yourself this gift as well—the gift of healing yourself—to make you whole and complete. You are looking at the world from a place of power and position of control for the first time in your life. Look at your family of origin. You, internally, are more solid than you have ever been."

"That is true, Colleen. But they had to nearly destroy me for it to happen." Her words were conciliatory.

"Maureen, you had to have a very major life crisis, and I would say that this is probably the most major life crisis anyone can go through."

Heartbroken, I cried, "I don't know if I will ever forgive him for this one! It's going to take a long time, Colleen."

"But that's okay, Maureen. It's important to recognize that you are not in denial. You are not saying everything's okay. You're setting boundaries. You don't know if you can forgive. Time is a factor here."

"Colleen, I'm not even going to guess at the time it will take to forgive him. I'm just going to take my damn time in healing. I know I still have to heal because I am the one with the wound. This was my life. To find out twenty-three years later you had someone else's child—" I collapsed into tears.

"That's an incredible shock," Colleen acknowledged compassionately, understanding my pain.

I told Colleen the story of nearly giving my son up for adoption when he was born. "Colleen, I left the hospital with him because I couldn't do that. I couldn't abandon him." There was incredible wisdom in Colleen's voice as she reassured me:

"You're very strong. You knew intuitively—you have always known—what is right for you—what is best for you."

"I couldn't leave him. I just couldn't leave him," I cried desolately.

"And now he has left you. He has abandoned you when you

didn't think this was going to happen."

"I didn't think he would have done this to me, Colleen. But I went back and read my diary, and things started to add up. He manipulated this whole thing to keep me out. He was behind it all. I think he has been behind what happened with my family to get attention and sympathy. I have no trust in him. He not only abandoned me, but also betrayed me behind my back for a very long time. And the realization has just made me sick." I told Colleen of the harsh e-mail I had sent Joseph.

"And now I have to protect myself, Colleen!" I said with a fierce determination.

"How did it feel when you sent that e-mail?" she asked.

"Good! Very, very powerful," I answered fervently. "He thinks he can laugh this one off, Colleen. No! This one will not be laughed off. He can't do it this time. I won't let him. And I will protect myself!"

"Just hear what you're saying," she cautioned.

"I have to protect myself. He will kill me. I know that now."

"Maureen, you have always been strong. Most women would have given up their child for adoption, and you're the first mother I have met who did not succumb to Social Services or the pressures of the doctors, the nurses, the stigmatization, the labeling—"

"Yes, there was a lot of labeling. I remember someone once said to me, 'You have an illegitimate son. You realize he's going to be called a bastard!'"

"Maureen, not only have you always been a strong woman, but you're also a risk-taker. When you have had to make an important decision for yourself, you made it in your best interests and in the best interests of your son. Even though you love and care deeply for him, you're at a point now where the cost to you is too high. You have made a choice now to say, 'I can't deal with this right now, Joey, because I need to protect me.' This is very major, Maureen."

"Colleen, I'm finally that strong person again who is saying, 'No more!'"

"No more. You have drawn the line. You have drawn the boundary. Just like when you said to that nurse, 'Give me my son!'

And your decision has come from a very strong place. You're protecting your place of wisdom—you know what you need."

"I needed my son. I could not abandon him. I couldn't do it."

"No. But at this point in time, you are also not prepared for the costs, both emotionally and physically, of having him in your life the way it has been. Because you're abandoning yourself, if you choose that route."

"Colleen, I have pushed him through the years to try and get an emotional reaction out of him. Something about him, emotionally, was not there."

"Maureen, you have set the boundary. You are now giving your son an opportunity. He can choose to grow or not to grow. You know as well as I do that we cannot force anyone to be, or feel, or act, the way we think they should. It's all about choices and how one chooses to live one's life."

"I choose to have him out of my life until I want him back in it," I said resolutely. "And that is coming from a position of real strength."

"And I would suggest that you probably haven't had a strong sense of guilt about saying the things you have said." She paused thoughtfully. "I sense some empowerment, Maureen."

"I feel no guilt about what I said in that e-mail, Colleen. And it was harsh. I want him to know this was serious. This was not a joke. And he wants to laugh it off."

"Well, you're being real. You're not denying what happened to you, and you need to be witnessed and validated. Joseph is a grown man with the ability to think and make choices, both emotional and physical, for his well-being. But you also have the right to make choices for your well-being, because if you don't, when you are pushed too far and are pretty close to going over that edge—"

"I was over the edge, Colleen!" I stressed unwaveringly.

"Then you know what the costs are. The costs of loving your son right now are just too high," she warned.

"Colleen, he saw me suffering and he turned his back on me through this whole thing again and again."

"He cannot be there to meet your emotional needs. He cannot be there to meet his own emotional needs," she confirmed.

"But this was too big for him to have turned his back on me. He saw me confused and in terrible pain and he laughed at me. He wanted this for himself, and in the end, he did push me over the edge, Colleen. I remember the day he turned his back and walked away from me and the pain I felt inside of me—" I convulsed in agonizing heartache.

"So you know pain then. And you also know about crisis—that it's an opportunity for you to live your life the way you want to live it. And no one can deny that you love your son and that he is connected to you. There is no way that that can ever be taken away. When we are pushed, however, and we have a high tolerance for pain, sometimes we need a major whammy for things to change because of that high tolerance for pain."

"Yes, I tolerated abuse from Joseph for years."

"Maureen, you have also tolerated abuse in your family of origin. That has been your role. That is what you have learned. So you have needed the Universe to say, '*Look, Maureen—wake up! This is your life! Be real!*' You have a right to be free in this world. So this is the big one—the major life transition and it hurts."

"Yet, Colleen, there were times when Joey was wonderful. If I had a dollar left and he wanted something, I would say, '*Joey, all I have is a dollar—that's all I have.*' And he would say, '*Mom, we don't need any money. We have each other!*' I will never forget he said that. So I would tell him, '*Well, a dollar is enough to get a couple of chocolate bars.*' And that's what we did. We splurged that last dollar on a little treat for ourselves. So we went through a lot of difficult times where there wasn't enough money."

"But the reality is—no one can take away the bond you have," Colleen assured me.

"Is there really a bond anymore?" I asked dismally.

"Of course there is! Right now stuff is happening. But it's happening for a reason, Maureen. And when you're in it, try to pull yourself up and look at it from a bigger perspective." She hesitated before proceeding:

"Maureen, you came from a dysfunctional family. You were a baby having a baby, but you fought the system. You were a survivor. You had child welfare workers in your home, watching every move you made. You learned how to tolerate pain. Years ago you made a decision that you believed was in both your and your son's best interests, just as this decision was, you believed, in his best interests—to find his birth father. So everything you have done has come from a place of best interests—a place of integrity."

"Colleen, I knew he would never find his sense of self unless he felt whole and complete and that that would not happen until the father came into the picture, so I thought: *I'm going to do it!*"

"And you did it! You had no control, however, over the outcome because you can't control variables. You can't control others. You don't know who they are or how they are going to react. The only thing you can do now is look at this as an opportunity for you to have your life. And to know and embrace you and the parts of you that have been hurt and alone and to reclaim them back. This is now about your time in your life, and how do you want to live the rest of it?" I was silent, lost in thought, as Colleen continued:

"Maureen, when you put all of the pieces together, it is like a tapestry. We're talking miracle stuff here."

"Colleen, for my eyes to have finally opened so that I could see the resemblance of my son to Bill—it took all those years."

"You could not completely fully see until the time was right. Maureen, when you were seventeen, you sacrificed your life to be a mother to your son. You needed all your strength to parent this little baby. You needed to get your basic needs met."

"I needed for us to survive. How could I also have dealt with the fact that I got pregnant through close contact with Bill? Colleen, I couldn't have handled that."

"Maureen, if you tried to deal with this stuff years ago, you would have been unable to cope. You would have been depressed, you would have been out of control, child welfare would have come and apprehended your son and placed him in foster care and you would have lost him.'

"Oh God, things were bad enough!" I cried in alarm.

"So that is why it had to wait. It had to wait until you were strong enough to be able to handle it," Colleen stressed firmly.

"Colleen, as it was, it nearly killed me now."

"So your defense mechanism kicked in so you could survive. So hear that! Everything has been from a place of protection for you to be able to survive and also to be a parent to the best of your ability. And we can't change things about how we parented. There are some things I wish I had done differently. But you do the best you can. And now you have a right to be who you are and have your life, Maureen."

"Colleen, I was security to my son. We did so many things together. There was a close bond—I don't know where it is now," I said dejectedly.

"But it's there. It's at a different place and stage. Now you have the added variable of the birth father who has completely added another dimension—another dynamic—to this."

"What does he mean to all of this? Does he really have importance?"

"Oh—significant importance," Colleen asserted.

"The birth father? Why?" I demanded obstinately.

"Because he is also part of who Joey is. The question is whether or not Joey can be at a place to understand what this means for him. He might be needing to re-create something that he never had. But there is an importance to know where we came from. Your goal through all of this was to give him a stronger sense of identity—of who he is."

"That will be achieved, whether it works out with Bill or not," I maintained.

"Yes. But the bottom line is, Joey's the one who's got to make that decision about the relationship." Reluctantly, I agreed.

"Maureen, it is about integration. Joseph needs to experience Bill as a human being because he has, in his own mind, created a fantasy. You have had the reality of your son, and you are getting more real all the time ... The masks are coming off, Maureen. Your dreams, your nightmares, are parts of you that need to get this stuff out. You're working so hard, Maureen. You're integrating and making sense of all the pieces." Thoughtfully, Colleen resumed:

"Maybe this is an opportunity for your son to work through stuff that he needs to work through, but it's also an opportunity for you to look at this from another viewpoint and say, 'Hey! *How in the heck did I do all this?*' You should be exhausted!" I stared at Colleen. Suddenly, the bizarreness of it all struck me, and I erupted into hysterical laughter.

"Do you think I'm not?" I asked her incredulously, still howling. Colleen persisted.

"I'm telling you—you should be exhausted! Physically, emotionally—" Cracking up, I interrupted her.

"Colleen, when the anti-depressants started to kick in, I was sleeping 15-16 hours a day."

"But that's important! You have held on so tight, Maureen. All of a sudden the elastic band goes *ping!*" Her analogy of the situation struck me as hilarious.

"There was a rope, I tied a knot in it and hung on!" I laughed hysterically at the mental imagery my own analogy conjured up. My infectious laughter filled the room and Colleen chuckled.

"But you did! For dear life! Not only for your life, but also for your son's life. And maybe if you look at it from a philosophical or a spiritual level—maybe there was a reason why you needed to be together—you and your son. Maybe you needed him. What would your life be like if you didn't have him when you were younger?"

"I would have been into drugs. I don't know that I would have survived." Wistfully, I paused. "Colleen, I still feel at some point I want to meet up with Bill, and I can't get rid of that feeling."

"But maybe that's okay. And maybe the timing is not right for that to happen, otherwise it would happen. You need more time for you. Bill may be in denial and be so disconnected—look what you're dealing with. Their reactions are predictable on one level because they are emotionally fearful—disconnected."

"Colleen, I have no respect for Bill," I said simply.

"And you don't have to. Maureen, you're protecting you. You don't need to go there."

"Oh, I don't want to now, at this point," I maintained.

"So what is time giving you?" she asked gently.

"Healing—I'm starting to heal from it, but it's going to take a long time. It still hurts. For me to have raised Bill's child and for Bill not to even acknowledge that or to acknowledge me as Joey's mother—that hurts!" I began to cry.

"Big time! And you know what? Those are your feelings and you have a right to grieve that."

"That hurts so badly. Because I knew Bill for years. We all hung out together—" I couldn't continue. The pain was unbearable.

"You're probably feeling discounted—invisible—and not worth anything. And that hurts, Maureen. Those are the things that need to be healed. You have a right to hurt that and to grieve that."

"I start getting fearful of things like Joey's graduation, his wedding, grandchildren. You know, Colleen? I'm thinking of all these things and it terrifies me."

"Sure! And what you do know is that you have never been better than you are right now. It's okay to think about those things, but it's also important to let yourself feel what you're feeling right now because time will sort it all out. And in time, you will know. Your whole life has been incredible, Maureen. You have not lived a normal life."

"It hasn't been very normal at all," I agreed.

"It has been exceptional. But you are also an exceptional woman because of your life experiences. You were a child having a child. You survived against all odds!" There was a quiet lull as Colleen reflected.

"You are also aware of the voice inside you. And when you wrote that e-mail to your son, it came from a place of protection, of wisdom. You have been processing this for a long time."

"Yes! I had to let him know I was onto his game. He knows this is serious now."

"Mom's pulled the plug," Colleen concluded.

"He thinks he can laugh and joke it away, Colleen. Not this time."

"And that's probably how he has coped through his life—through laughing or minimizing—because of the pain of the emotional abandonment he went through. That's one of his defenses—his coping mechanism."

"I understand that. But at the same time, he still had a wonderful mother who was there for him, and I haven't been given enough recognition for that. I took all his pain, all his anger, all his abuse."

"But what you're saying is you don't want it anymore."

"No—I'm not taking it anymore!" I repeated fiercely.

"But nobody else was there for him, Maureen. You have been it."

"So I had to take all his pain, all his anger, all his abuse?"

"And that happens—until you can't do it anymore. The support is no longer there. The support is gone. And you need this time." I lapsed into silence for several moments. There was a calm, yet beautiful, strength and forcefulness to my voice.

"I need this time and I'm taking this time, and I will not be there for any kind of support for my son."

"So hear what you're saying!" Colleen cautioned. "'I'm taking this time because I need this time.'"

The session was over. As I pondered over all that had been said, a powerful and poignant awareness came to me. *Thank God I had found Colleen. When so many others didn't know the way, I had found Colleen.*

Colleen knew the way.

17   *The Journey Home*

December arrived. Christmas was fast approaching and the thought filled me with unspeakable grief.

There would be no shopping for Christmas presents this year, nor would there be any turkey or unwrapping of ornaments or search for a tree. In effect, there was nothing to celebrate and no reason for a celebration. Dismally, I watched the hordes of people gathering in the malls, scurrying frantically from store to store. *The fools! Didn't they realize Christmas was just another day?*

To my surprise, Joseph's girlfriend Becki telephoned.

"Maureen, Joe wants to move out real bad. He hates living in a house with six people. He has to pay $250.00 a month for rent." *What happened to all the support Bill had promised his son? I thought ruefully.*

Filled with trepidation, I asked Becki how Joseph's relationship was going with Bill. She answered pensively:

"Maureen, they will never be father and son or parent and child—only friends. Bill acts like a twenty-five-year-old kid and goes to the bar all the time." I felt a smattering of relief. It was as I had thought it would be. She continued:

"They have the same mannerisms and you can tell they're related." Becki's words tore at my heart and I began to cry.

"Becki, that is what I needed to see." She seemed to understand and, unlike my son, asked me how I was.

"Becki, there was a lot of damage done to me. I haven't healed yet. I'm still living in the fantasy—in the dream—and it hurts." Becki quietly said she understood.

"Maureen, Joe shouldn't have to choose between you and Bill." Her words stung sharply and I was upset with her naiveté.

"Becki, it isn't about choosing. Joe turned his back on me when I needed him most."

"Maureen, he did that because he wanted this for himself. He was afraid that he would not see Bill if you had gotten involved. Joey said that you've fought before and that this would blow away." I was stunned. *So my son was counting on this just blowing away?*

"No, Becki. This is different. I'm no longer capable of taking his abuse or his lies." Becki appeared to understand and, not surprisingly, told me she was leaving Calgary in two days and moving to Vancouver. She was going to look for an apartment with Joseph so that he could afford to leave Bill's house.

I cried for several hours when I got off the phone. My son didn't get his dream, and worse, Bill was not the man of integrity I had so desperately hoped for.

Finally, it was the afternoon of December 24. It was a very difficult day at work, side-stepping questions from co-workers about my plans for the holidays. I was relieved when the day finally ended and I could go home.

There was a message from Joseph on the answering machine. *Mom, I'll be in town on the 27th if you want to get together with me.*

All evening I foolishly kept wishing my son would just walk through the door and everything would be okay. I was torn between seeing him and not seeing him, knowing in my heart it was not a good idea to see him. I had only wanted an apology from him, and I couldn't back down on my long-fought boundaries now. To do so would be catastrophic for my health. I would lose any ground I had gained in my long, drawn-out struggle to put an end to our toxic, abusive relationship.

It was indeed a very lonely night. Unable to sleep, I listened to a tape recording of one of Colleen's sessions. Again and again I rewound the tape. Her soothing voice finally lulled me to sleep.

Christmas Day arrived. It had snowed heavily throughout the night, and a fresh blanket of snow covered everything in sight.

So it was Christmas Day! It was just another damn day! And it would be a quiet day. Joseph had promised that he would be home for Christmas. He had lied.

The day wore on. Forlornly, I pondered over everything that had happened. I knew I was no longer capable of returning to a severely dysfunctional relationship with my son and that I had to protect myself at all costs. As Colleen had stressed to me again and again, the costs of loving my son were just too high. And God only knows I had seen the other side and knew the destruction that lay there. Joseph had Bill now, and he was more than willing to throw me away in the process. That was fine with me. He would have to live with his choices, and I would have to live with mine.

Finally, it was 6 p.m. on a long and lonely Christmas Day. Somehow, the thought of cooking a turkey for one was just too much to bear, and I had decided weeks earlier to prepare a prime rib dinner. Late in the afternoon, I had gone for what I thought would be an invigorating walk in the crisp blanket of snow, but the sight of families joyously gathered in brightly-lit homes filled me with a terrible melancholy. My eyes stung with tears and I hurried home through the deep snow, snowflakes gently falling around me.

In the midst of cooking dinner, I was struck by an overpowering feeling of anxiety and was unable to shake the feeling. *Something was wrong!* Suddenly, I had to know where Joseph was.

Consumed with the feeling, I called Becki, who had come home to her parents for Christmas. Her father informed me Joe wasn't there and that he had stayed in Vancouver for the holidays. I hung up the phone, thinking how lonely my son must be out there in B.C., all by himself. My heart ached for him.

Then Becki called. Brightly, she wished me a Merry Christmas. "Becki, is Joe there with you?" She was surprised at my question.

"Didn't he tell you?" Gripped with a sense of foreboding, I asked her uneasily:

"Tell me what?"

"He went skiing to Whistler. Joey, Bill and Laurie—they went skiing for three days. Didn't he call you and tell you?"

I couldn't hear another word.

"Well, Becki, at least now I know what his priorities are. He promised me he would come home for Christmas. Do you remember that walk we took in the woods, Becki, before he left? He promised me over and over he would be home for Christmas." Becki quietly answered that she remembered.

I was upset, angry and confused and began to cry. "Well, he's hurt me again. I can't take any more. All I wanted was an apology, Becki. I never want to see him again!" Becki was silent.

"It's your turn now, Becki. I wish you luck and I wish you all the best." Becki, poor thing, was indeed shocked and timidly said good-bye.

I got off the phone and cried. My soul wept in heartbreaking agony. My son had done it to me again. He put Bill and that horrible woman ahead of me after I had repeatedly warned him never to do that again. He had promised me and once again he had lied. I phoned my good friend Julie and wept profusely to her. I was hysterical and poor Julie did her best to calm me down.

It all made sense now. Joseph had cleverly called at 3:30 p.m. the previous afternoon, just before he left for the mountains with Bill and Laurie. He needed to cover his tracks so that I wouldn't suspect anything. My son knew how ill I had been, yet none of that seemed to matter to him. He lacked empathy, compassion and understanding and could only think of himself. He could never see or understand my pain.

I didn't want him back in my life. It was more important for him to be with Bill and Laurie for Christmas Day while his mother was ill and alone. That hurt so very, very badly. I wept into my prime rib dinner and, unable to eat, morosely packed up the food and called it a day.

At 10:45 p.m., I was startled to hear the phone ring. It was Joe. I didn't give him a chance to utter a word and yelled:

"So it was more important for you to go skiing with Bill and that horrible woman rather than come home and see your Mom for Christmas!" He managed to say:

"I called you yesterday—" Furious, I cut him off.

"I told you never to put that woman ahead of me again—and you did! You've hurt me again! No more! You won't hurt me again!

He snarled sarcastically, "Whatever!"

"Stay out of my life!" I shouted and slammed down the phone. He had once again proved himself to be just as selfish and insensitive as he had always been. Once again, he had succeeded in hurting me beyond words. Sobbing uncontrollably, I crawled into bed. Sometime during the night I awoke, screaming in terror.

The full-blown depression was back.

Boxing Day arrived. I struggled to get out of bed and decided to fight the Boxing Day crowds, thinking it might do me some good to get out and about. Amongst the throngs of wall-to-wall people, no one noticed me or the sadness that permeated the depths of my soul. Jostled from store to store, I purchased a few items for myself. Anything I bought, I bought for me. It was certainly not what I was used to. I treated myself to whatever I wanted, and my spirits began to lift.

The next day I was promptly in Dr. Narsui's office. I told him how hurt I was that my son spent Christmas with Bill. He was very gentle with me and explained:

"Maureen, your son has always seen you as his anchor or rock and has always known he could come back and attach to you anytime he wanted. You have always been there. In a way, it's a compliment that he always comes back to you."

Tearfully, I replied, "Dr. Narsui, I can't take it anymore. I need to break the bond. I don't want to be my son's mother anymore." My words shocked Dr. Narsui, and he responded with kindness and compassion.

"Maureen, that's not true. You love your son, and you don't really want to break the bond. It is time for you to break free."

"Dr. Narsui, I need to break free, but I need my son out of my life so I can heal. I still haven't healed from the other pain, and I have more to deal with. I can't deal with this anymore. That anchor has to be taken away from my son to teach him he can't continue to take advantage of me as he has been doing for years." Dr. Narsui agreed.

"Maureen, tell your son you'll talk to him in six months, and in the meantime, you will take the time to heal. Your son has taken advantage of you for a very long time, and he has not shown you any appreciation for what you have done over the years. He needs to learn that he cannot do that anymore." He continued:

"I know if something happened, you would be the first one there to help your son. It's what a mother feels in her heart." I knew Dr. Narsui was right and I burst into tears. I would die for my son, I loved him so much. I told Dr. Narsui that hearing my son's voice alone triggered a depression. He was firm and very concerned.

"Maureen, this has to stop. You have to stay away from your son for six months to a year to heal."

He increased my medication to counteract the breakthrough depression and I left, feeling somewhat brighter.

The following day, a little voice inside of me kept whispering, *'It's going to be okay. It's going to be okay.'* I kept hearing the voice over and over and wondered with perplexity what it meant. It was a freezing -32°F outside, and feeling somewhat revived, I donned heavy winter boots and winter apparel, shoveled the walks and trekked through the deep snow to the store and back. The air was crisp and fresh, and amazingly, I began to feel a little better.

The phone rang at 5:30 p.m. It was Joe again, at Becki's old place in Calgary. I stood there, transfixed. Why on earth would he dare call me after what I had said to him? Obviously, he had not taken me seriously. The message was clear on the machine.

"Hi there! It's just me. I'm at Becki's if you want to get in touch with me. I'll be dropping off a little something that I got you for Christmas even though you—"

Angrily, I grabbed the phone and in a strong, clear voice, cut him off.

"No! Don't you dare! I don't want it!"

"It's too late. I already got it—" I interrupted him again, furious.

"No! I don't want it and I don't want to see you! Every time I hear your voice, it triggers another depression and I end up in doctors' and therapists' offices! I don't want anything from you! I'm still trying to heal from the pain of being left out of the reunion, and then you go skiing with Bill and Laurie for Christmas!" Joe answered nastily, but I could hear a trailing anxiousness in his voice:

"Mother, you wouldn't even talk to me before Christmas!"

"I asked you again and again for an apology. That's all I asked for. You have your life, and I have mine! Stay away from me!"

I hung up the phone, not quite believing what I had just said. Joseph would be hopping mad now. Poor Becki. He would probably take it out on her. I felt powerful, so incredibly powerful. *I'm going to be okay. I have to protect myself. I will protect myself.*

And I had done just that.

I did not feel bad about what I had said. *Was I finally free of his emotional dependency on me? Free of a severely co-dependent relationship? Was this the emotional break Dr. Narsui had spoken of?*

It was January and the start of a new year. In another long counseling session with Colleen, she agreed my son needed therapy and that Bill and Laurie had been blatant about having Joey with them for Christmas.

Joey was the only child Bill would likely ever have, and Laurie had wanted so badly to have his child. By denying my identity, it was possible for her to deny that part of my son's identity as well, enabling her to fulfill the fantasy that Joey was her and Bill's child. Colleen interrupted my thoughts.

"Maureen, I could help your son, but I feel that some sessions with both of you would be good. You know all the trouble you have been having with your family? Your son has been behind it all."

I groaned, recognizing the truth.

"Maureen, he will say anything to make you look bad." Incredulous, I asked her:

"Why?"

"Because he doesn't feel good about himself, and by making you look bad, he gets more attention."

"Colleen, he's sick!"

"Well, no, but I would say that he's complex, complicated." I told Colleen of our traumatic bonding and that I felt I had come through it, but he hadn't.

"Colleen, Joseph has always repressed his emotions and depended on me for them—something which I can no longer do. That's why I have always felt sorry for him—because I have always known that emotionally, something was wrong."

"You bandaged up his pain, Maureen. He really needed to feel that pain, especially when he was little and both of you were traumatized. There will either be a big crisis soon, or Joseph will dissociate and never feel anything." Her words filled me with apprehension for the future. *Would my son remain emotionally detached and repressed for the rest of his life?* I left Colleen's office, reeling with overwhelming anxiety.

A week passed and I saw Dr. Narsui again. I sat and wept through our visit. He took a harder line with me.

"Maureen, you're at the wall. You must go through the wall alone and leave your son behind. You cannot take your son with you, and you cannot change him." We spoke of possessiveness, and Dr. Narsui asked if I felt that way towards my son.

"No, I'm not possessive of him. I just want him to get some therapy." Dr. Narsui firmly disagreed.

"Maureen, that is your son's problem. It is not for you to solve."

"But without therapy, the relationship will remain abusive," I argued.

"Then you must face the fact that it can indeed happen. Your son may decide not to look at his past, and he may never change." His words shook me. The truth was hard to hear and so very hard to accept.

My son had turned into Bill. Despite the fact my son had never known his father, he had turned into him anyway.

I cried in alarm, "Dr. Narsui, if that happens, I cannot have a relationship with my son because it would always be abusive!"

"Maureen, you have to get to a stage where nothing your son does will bother you." *Surely, he was joking. How could such a thing be possible?*

"Are you spiritual, Maureen?" he asked me, to which I answered, "Yes."

"Nothing is more powerful than God. Pray to God to help you through this." Miserably, I told him that I had prayed for hundreds of hours and that it hadn't helped.

"Don't stop praying, Maureen. You will be heard." I sat there—crushed, broken, destroyed.

"Maureen, we come into this world alone, and we leave alone. When you change, everyone else will change around you."

"Dr. Narsui, I don't know how to get through the wall!" I wailed despairingly.

"It's a process. It will happen, naturally."

I had to continue on the journey, alone. I couldn't help my son. I left Dr. Narsui's office, feeling so very sad.

I've lost him. I've lost my son.

It was hard to go back to work. I wept throughout the night, realizing that Joseph might not change and that our relationship could be over for good. Joseph had counted on my undying, unconditional love for him always being there. It wasn't.

Sleep continued to evade me.

Day after day, I continued to drag myself in to work—pale, drawn and feeling and looking like death. Several of my co-workers were gathered one morning, chatting by the receptionist's desk.

"I'm dying. I'm dying a slow, excruciating death," I told them. "Can't you tell?" They stared at me in horror.

It was mid-January of another bleak and sorrowful year. Something had to be done. I could not continue to live as I had been doing. The time had come to end it all. It was time to make the journey home.

I was going to see Bill.

Speaking to Colleen, she said, "It's a very healthy thing to do and a very difficult thing to do, and it will take a great deal of courage.

You are doing this for you. This has nothing to do with your son. You know what you need, and this is best for you. Do you have something to take on your journey?"

"Yes! I have my favorite sweater and running shoes to change into. They feel like home."

"Yes, that's what I meant. Maureen, I'm going to play devil's advocate. What will you do if Bill refuses to see you?"

"It doesn't matter. I'll insist. I'll do whatever it takes. I just need to see him." She commended me, wished me well on my journey and told me to call from Vancouver if I needed her. I thanked her and assured her I would call if I needed to. I was so thankful Colleen understood. It was time to get everything over with before it took my life.

Thursday arrived. I was extremely nervous at work and confided my intentions to a few select co-workers, not wanting to hear any rebuke or admonishment for what I was about to do. I spoke to Murray and he was wonderful and wished me well on my trip. He was such a kind and caring man and had comforted me through many dismal days at the office. He knew how tough the trip was going to be on me.

Tomorrow is the day. Tomorrow it will all be over. Finally, work was finished and it was time to go home. Carefully, I packed my change of clothes and checked them at least ten times to make sure I didn't forget anything. I was a nervous wreck and was filled with a tremendous anxiety and prayed like I had never prayed before. Unable to sleep, I stayed up until 1:30 a.m. before I finally went to bed. There were intermittent bouts of sleep as I tossed and turned all night. The alarm went off at 4:30 a.m.

It was January 17, 1997. The Big Day had finally arrived.

Mercifully, I managed to get out of bed without falling back to sleep. Of all the days of my life, this one was too important a day to sleep in. After showering and dressing, it was time to go. I looked good, despite the lack of sleep. Barely having eaten for days, I had lost several more pounds and fit nicely into my black suit. I was at the airport by 6:15 a.m., more than an hour prior to departure.

God, let everything go well! Let me finally make the journey home! I prayed fervently.

As I made every effort to stay calm, I knew in my heart I could handle myself with the utmost of dignity and integrity on what would be the most difficult experience I would ever know in my lifetime.

God, accompany me on this journey and help me through it. Let Bill be there this morning so that I may finally find peace. Should anything go wrong and I do not meet him, I make a contract this hour, this minute, this second, with myself, to let this go. I will accept it as God's wish for me, and I will accept it as best I can.

It was time to go to the departure gate. *Remember what Julie said—stay calm, complacent and in control.* I kept repeating Julie's message to myself, over and over.

The hot cup of tea served to me on the plane was soothing and helped calm me. The cabin lights in the plane were dimmed, and a beautiful, shimmering line of tiny ceiling lights lined the length of the darkened plane. Outside the window, through the blackness, I could see tiny farmhouses dotting the landscape far below me. Little lights were on in little houses, and I wondered what other people were doing on this most important day of all days—the day that I was making my journey home.

It was dismal and dark as we arrived in Vancouver and the plane taxied to a stop. A steady, cold, drizzling rain was falling. Having no luggage except my knapsack, I was able to quickly catch a taxi to Cambie and Georgia Streets.

Inside Bill's office building, I fought to remain calm. Feeling overwhelmingly stressed, I checked and re-checked my appearance in the mirror in the ladies' room on the ground floor. *What if Bill didn't recognize me? I thought in horror. What if I didn't recognize him? What on earth would I do then? Stop it! Stop it! Everything's going to be okay! Everything's going to be okay!*

I took one final, deep breath and left the safety and security of the washroom and proceeded to the fourth floor. Feeling very calm and looking very business-like, I approached the girl at the window and told her I was in town for business for the day and had dropped by to see Bill for a few moments. As luck would have it, he had yet to arrive at work. She told me to take a seat and that Bill would be there shortly.

"Is there another door to the office?" I asked innocently. I remembered my last harrowing trip to this place and how Bill had effectively eluded me.

"No, Bill will come through that door right there."

Patiently, I waited. Several minutes passed and I noticed the girls whispering and glancing at me inquisitively from behind the large glass window. No doubt they were wondering who I was.

The door opened and a tall, rather large, man entered. He wasn't exceptionally handsome, but attractive nevertheless. Thankfully, I recognized him. It was indeed Bill. Nearly twenty years had passed, but I knew immediately it was him. He glanced at me and I promptly stood up. Bravely, and mustering all the courage I possessed, I spoke to him.

"Hello, Bill. I'm here on business for the day, and I came by to drop off these pictures for you."

He smiled. *I recognized that smile. That alluring, charming smile hadn't changed.*

"Come on in here." He gestured to an adjoining office a few feet away. I wasn't sure he knew who I was.

"Do you know who you're speaking to, Bill?" I asked him. "Do you recognize me?"

"Yes, I know who you are," he answered confidently.

He led me to a small room and told me he would be right back. I sat down and felt a beautiful calmness overcome me. I removed the several photographs of Joey I had brought and lay them on the table. I had meticulously put together a small photo album of Joey's school photographs, from kindergarten through grade 12.

Bill returned. He looked over the pictures and was obviously pleased. We spoke for a while and I tried to put him at ease.

"Why don't you call Joe? Does he know you're here?" Bill asked, concerned.

"No, Bill. Joseph has abused me for the last eight years, and I can't take it anymore. My son is controlling, manipulative and abusive and lies behind my back. I was a very loving, nurturing mother to him, and I deserve to be treated with respect. We all do." Bill agreed.

"I don't want him in my life. Not until he changes and can give me respect. We're parents of the same child and there is a connection—a bond—and we can work together, Bill." Again, Bill agreed.

"I know what you mean. We're having problems with Laurie's girl right now."

"Bill, Joe is too old for this. He's twenty-four years old and he has to grow up. He has hurt me badly, and I just can't take it anymore." Bill acknowledged that he understood but sounded perturbed.

"Well he can't stay with us!" The abruptness of his tone surprised me.

"Perhaps he's overstayed his welcome, Bill."

"It's not that! It's just that it's really crowded and we don't have the room."

We continued talking. It was an incredibly beautiful and healing experience, sitting across from Bill, my son's father. I glanced at Bill's hands and recognized them. They were my son's hands. And Bill had thumbs that turned slightly upwards, just as my son's did. There were similarities in the face. The eyes and eyebrows were the same. And he combed his hair back as Joe did. It was all there.

I had come home. I had come home at last.

Bill had not seemed to have done much with his life. I detected a note of embarrassment in his voice as he averted his gaze, unable to boast of any accomplishments or achievements. Part of me felt sorry for him. He was the same young man I had known in high school. He hadn't really changed—he hadn't grown up at all.

Fifteen minutes later it was time to go.

"Maureen, you timed this really well. If you had come here any other day, we wouldn't have been here. We're packing up and moving the office today to Burnaby." *My timing had become impeccable.*

I stood up, ready to leave. "How about a hug?" I said jovially to Bill.

He came towards me and we hugged for several seconds. Bill held me so tightly I could barely breathe. Choked up with emotion, I let out a small cry and managed to say:

"You gave me a beautiful son, Bill, and I thank you for that!"

He let go of me and I held his face in my hands and gently pulled him towards me. I kissed his mouth and he responded. It was a beautiful moment. And it was all mine.

"Bill, you don't have to be afraid of me."

"I'm not afraid of you!" he answered defensively. But I knew he was. He was terrified of me and of the past that I reminded him of— a past that he had not yet had the courage to face.

Sailing on air, I left his office and changed into my clothes downstairs in the ladies' room. It felt good to get out of my business outfit and into comfortable walking clothes. Following Bill's instructions, I headed towards the Bay downtown to purchase a lovely, red umbrella.

It was indeed the most wonderful day of my life and an experience I would never forget. Bursting with exuberance, I wandered happily around downtown in the rain and called Murray from the Vancouver Hotel. Exhilarated, I told him how wonderful the visit went. He was happy for me and congratulated me and told me to roam around Robson Street—that I would enjoy it.

Dressed warmly, I spent the day visiting my gallery and shops on the Island. I stopped in at *Harry's* on Robson Street for a huge, delicious turkey sandwich and equally scrumptious pecan salad. Unable to eat it all, I carefully tucked it away in my knapsack. Outside, homeless people sat in the cold, drizzling rain, hands outstretched. I gave money to all I could, until I ran out. Then I gave away my food. It was a day to give whatever I could. I had been given a blessed day, a remarkable day that would go a long way in healing my broken spirit, and I could afford to give back.

Soaring on a cloud, the day finally came to a close as I sat in a crowded Market Square, sipping a hot cup of tea and watching the rain pour down. Gulls flew about and swooped down to pick at bits of bread thrown to them. Enchanting music from a mandolin floated lazily through the air, and I sat there—warm, contented and watching the ocean and the world around me. I was back. Back in the land of the living, and it felt good.

Exhausted from the trip, I slept for eighteen beautiful hours that night, awakening at 4 p.m. Seven hours later, I was back in bed and slept another fourteen hours.

What was that noise? What was that strange sound breaking the beautiful, peaceful silence of the night?

It was laughter.

I was laughing in my sleep.

18 *The Gift of Wisdom*

Two and a half years passed.

The road had been long and the way difficult, but I had survived.

As I prepared for what would be my final visit with Dr. Narsui, I thought about all that he had done for me to bring me to this point in my life. Together with Colleen, he had helped me work through a very difficult process that had seen me propelled back to a traumatic and violent childhood and wounds that had never healed. Together with Colleen, he had forced me to see and accept the truth.

For so long, I had maintained the roles and expectations that others had for me and which I needed in order to survive in a family as dysfunctional as mine was. Having reclaimed my life, I would no longer play any role or live by anyone else's values, beliefs, misconceptions or preconceptions. I had found my truth and was proud to have done so. And I would be silenced no more.

For so many years I had fought abuse, but now, through the grace of God, I could feel that abuse. And the depths of my pain had been great. It was only in the depths of that pain that I had been able to see truth. And the truth was that I had not been living an authentic life. I had not known how to love me.

Through the journey, I became strong. I would no longer tolerate abuse, nor would I ever go back to it. I no longer needed chaos or trauma in my life to survive. For to live with those things was to live an empty and meaningless life.

Joseph and I had reconciled, but the reconciliation had been brief. I had changed dramatically, and he could not understand, nor could he fully accept, the changes that had occurred in me. He was where I could not be, and the deep chasm that separated us swelled and widened with each mounting conflict with him.

It was as if I were standing on the shore, waving to him on a ship as it pulled away from shore. As the vessel sailed out to sea, the distance between us grew until I could no longer see him, and he could no longer see me. I called to him, but he could no longer hear me.

My heart ached for my son. But I knew this was now his journey and one which he had to travel alone.

I had tried desperately to teach him, but he was not willing to learn. I had stood by his side, but he could not stand by me. Without loyalty or trust, we had nothing. He had not nurtured the love I had so abundantly given him, and it had nearly been destroyed. But I had loved him more than life itself, and I knew that my love for him would endure. At times I wondered if I had given and loved too much. But in reality, I knew I had had the love to give.

It was now time to give to myself and to love me.

In taking the journey home, I had come home to myself.

Although I cared deeply for my mother, I had to release her and let her go. She was still cloaked in shame, and I could not rip her blanket from her. She would be cold and she would not survive.

Nor would I be lured back into the shadows, where truth disappeared and secrecy, lies and denial hid in the darkness. I had stood in my truth, and truth was where I had to be.

Just as I bore the wounds from my own childhood, so had my son.

I hoped that one day he would see and come to terms with what had happened to him and how it had affected his life. I prayed that one day he would embrace compassion and empathy and no longer be blind to the pain he caused others.

In seeking out the truth, I had stepped out of the shadows, out of the darkness, into the light. Here, the colours danced with vibrancy, their distinctions clear. There were no distortions or indistinctness here in the light. Everything was clear—brilliant—true.

I was no longer afraid.

Peace had come to me at last.

Bibliography

The Primal Wound: Understanding the Adopted Child, by Nancy Newton Verrier, MFCC. Gateway Press, Baltimore, MD, 1993.

Which Way You Goin' Billy, by Susan Jacks. The Poppy Family, 1970.

The Holy Bible.

Article in Washington Post, reprinted in Calgary Herald March 28, 1998, by Shawn Johnston, forensic psychologist, Sacramento, California.

Recommended Reading

The Primal Wound: Understanding the Adopted Child, by Nancy Newton Verrier, MFCC. Gateway Press, Baltimore, MD, 1993.

Facing Love Addiction: Giving Yourself the Power to Change the Way You Love, by Pia Mellody, author of *Facing Codependence* with Andrea Wells Miller and J. Keith Miller. HarperSanFrancisco, 1992.

Facing Codependence, by Pia Mellody with Andrea Wells Miller and J. Keith Miller, HarperSanFrancisco, 1989.

The Language of Letting Go, by Melody Beattie, Author of Codependent No More and Beyond Codependency. Hazelden Foundation, 1990.

Codependent No More: How to Stop Controlling Others and Start Caring for Yourself, by Melody Beattie. Hazelden Foundation, 1987, 1992.

Healing the Child Within, by Charles L. Whitfield, M.D. Health Communications, Inc., Deerfield Beach, Florida, 1987.

A Gift To Myself, by Charles L. Whitfield, M.D. Health Communications, Inc., Deerfield Beach, Florida, 1990.

Boundaries and Limits in Relationships and Recovery, by Charles L. Whitfield, M.D. Health Communications, Inc., Deerfield Beach, Florida, 1991.

The Family: A Revolutionary Way of Self-Discovery, by John Bradshaw. Health Communications, Inc., Deerfield Beach, Florida, 1988.

Healing the Shame That Binds You, by John Bradshaw. Health Communications, Inc., Deerfield Beach, Florida, 1988.

Family Secrets: What You Don't Know Can Hurt You, by John Bradshaw. Bantam Books, New York, 1995.

For Your Own Good: Hidden Cruelty In Child-Rearing And The Roots Of Violence, by Alice Miller. Farrar Strauss Giroux, New York, 1983.

The Road Less Traveled: A New Psychology of Love, Traditional Values and Spiritual Growth, by M. Scott Peck, M.D. Simon & Schuster, New York, 1978.

Real Boys, by William S. Pollack, Ph.D. Clinical psychologist and co-director of the Center for Men at McLean Hospital/Harvard Medical School, an assistant clinical professor of psychiatry at the Harvard Medical School. Random House, Inc., New York, 1998.

Adult Children: The Secrets of Dysfunctional Families, by John Friel, Ph.D. & Linda Friel, M.A. Health Communications, Inc., Deerfield Beach, Florida, 1988.

An Adult Child's Guide to What's "Normal," by John Friel, Ph.D. & Linda Friel, M.A. Health Communications, Inc., Deerfield Beach, Florida, 1990.

When Words are Not Enough: The Women's Prescription for Depression and Anxiety, by Valerie Davis Raskin, M.D. Broadway Books, New York, 1997.